Best Wishes

Love

courage!

Keep

D0031338

8-1

ONE
STEP
AT A TIME

LENOR MADRUGA

ONE STEP AT A TIME

A young woman's inspiring struggle to walk again.

McGRAW-HILL BOOK COMPANY

New York   St. Louis   San Francisco
Düsseldorf   Mexico   Toronto

1 2 3 4 5 6 7 8 9   D O D O   7 8 3 2 1 0 9

LIBRARY OF CONGRESS CATALOGING IN PUBLICATION DATA
Madruga, Lenor.
  One step at a time.
  1. Hemipelvectomy—Biography.   2. Physically
handicapped—United States—Biography.   3. Madruga, Lenor.
I. Title.
RD549.M24   362.4'3'0926 [B]   79-9975
ISBN 0-07-039459-8

Book design by Marsha Picker

To God for his miracle
and to my husband for his love

My warmest thanks and acknowledgments to:

Dr. Muriel James, my stepmother, for encouraging me
 to write my story;

Ernie Brawley, my brother, for saying, "Forget the
 ghostwriter!";

John Brockman, my agent, for believing in me;

Peggy Tsukahira, my editor, for refining my sometimes
 ambiguous and redundant writing;

Joe Madruga, my husband, for patiently reviewing
 each draft of the manuscript;

Dr. "Lowery," Dr. Glover, and Dr. Eltherington, with
 special thanks to Dr. Brakovec and Fred Karg;

Evelyn Reed, my tireless secretary, for all the work and
 fun;

and all my special friends who generously gave me
 hours of their time and energy.

Contents

The verses at the beginning of each chapter and the title for Chapter 6 come from I Am a Woman Who . . . *by Ann McNair with photographs by Marilyn Robertson. Ann McNair died of cancer on December 29, 1977.*

Why Me?

It was my birthday, Friday, March 22, 1974. I was a fashion model, the wife of a rancher, and the mother of two little girls. I found a hard lump on my left leg. As a result, within a month, I had lost my leg and part of my hip. In the process I found myself. I survived, my family survived . . . only God knows how.

Let me begin with that day, my thirty-second birthday.

Each year when my birthday rolls around I'm filled with a sense of excitement. Like a little kid anticipating her first birthday party. That's why I just couldn't wait for that day, Friday, March 22, 1974, to begin. After ushering my family off in the morning—husband to the fields for spring sugarbeet planting, oldest daughter to grammar school and youngest to nursery school—I was off to meet the day.

At noon I was to produce and model in a spring fashion show; later, a lunch in my honor with husband and friends.

The fashion show went well that day. Over the past four years, I had been involved in modeling and producing fashion shows at local hotels, using some professional models, but mostly housewives and star-struck teenagers. Some of my best models were women over fifty, who had already raised their children and were now looking for something to do for themselves, some form of personal excitement.

I had become interested in modeling quite by chance. I was having lunch at a local hotel where a fashion show happened to be in progress. That year afternoon fashion shows were a very popular source of entertainment throughout the state. After the show, the coordinator came up and asked if I'd like to model for her. I was flattered, and agreed.

After two months of working for her, I decided to produce my own shows. I certainly had enough attractive friends to start with, and I knew most of the merchants in town. The first show was held in Tracy in our oldest, most charming hotel. Within a year, I was producing shows in other towns as well. As a direct result of my fashion shows, I was asked to write a weekly column for the *Tracy Press* that not only discussed fashion, but also included social trivia.

Champagne was flowing during lunch and I was surrounded by many friends who faithfully attended the Friday afternoon fashion shows. Barney Caruso, the hotel's owner, proposed a toast: "To Lenor on her thirty-second birthday. May her career in modeling, producing, and writing continue to soar."

At home that evening, while enjoying a hot bath, I reflected on the joys of my life at thirty-two. I was still deliriously in love with my husband after ten years of marriage. I had two healthy, lovely little daughters. I had just completed the restoration of an old two-story home that we had moved 28 miles downriver on a barge. And to top it off, I was enjoying a career in fashion. On that day, March 22, 1974, life was good, totally fulfilling. I was young, attractive, healthy, and a sense of inextinguishable expectation flowed within me.

After soaking for half an hour in the hot bath, I began to wash. I ran the soap over my body, enjoying its delicious, slippery feel until that moment . . . that indescribable moment when I felt something unusual on the inside of my left thigh. I felt again, probing, a little confused by its sudden hardness and bigness. "Oh, perhaps it's just fat," I thought. . . . No, it was a lump, a very distinct, very hard lump. It didn't hurt and it wasn't tender, it was just there, solid and immobile. I could hear my two daughters romping in their bedroom and decided it was about time to get out of the bath. A mother of a two-year-old and a five-year-old can never linger long in the bathtub. Besides, my tranquil bath had suddenly turned disquieting. I dried myself quickly, checked on the girls, and hurried downstairs to have Joseph, my husband, check the lump to assure me that it was nothing. Suddenly, with a sigh of relief, I remembered that I had cut my foot the other night at a dance. Someone had gotten a little boisterous and accidentally had kicked me. "Thank God," I moaned, "it's just a gland swelling up due to the cut on my foot." Joseph agreed. Nevertheless, I decided to check with Dr. Brakovec in the

5

morning. After tucking my little girls in for the night, I headed for my bedroom to get dressed for bed. Just as I reached the doorway, an unnerving feeling of foreboding came over me. Something was about to happen over which I had no control.

I looked around our large and airy Victorian bedroom. It was all freshly painted and decorated in soft blues and beiges. I was delighted with the job of restoration that we had accomplished. For too many years it had suffered the indignities of neglect. Somehow, I had always felt at peace when I was in this room. Not so on that particular warm spring night of my thirty-second birthday. Suddenly, I found myself on my knees, like a child, hands clasped, entreating God: "Please let the lump be nothing!"

The following morning I called the doctor. He agreed that it was probably nothing, but he would be happy to check it. Because it was Saturday, his offices were closed, so I would have to meet him in the emergency room at the hospital. I dropped the children off at my mother-in-law's house and planned to do my grocery shopping after my brief stop at the hospital.

I checked in with the nurse at the front desk. She asked me to sign the usual questionnaire. I tried to explain that I only had a minute and it was just a little old lump I wanted checked, probably an infection. One of our local doctors passed by me while I was standing at the reception counter. Four years ago, when my eldest daughter, Christianna, was six months old, he had treated her for a very serious virus. Dr. Hogan greeted me and said, "How do you keep such a trim figure? You look great!" That was all I needed, a doctor's reassurance that I was fine. What was I doing wasting my time at the emergency room of Tracy Hospital, signing all those endless papers? I thanked the nurse and said that I was being silly and didn't want to waste her or the good doctor's time checking a ridiculous lump that suddenly had decided to manifest itself on my left thigh. Abruptly, I excused myself. I couldn't get out of that sterile, antiseptic room fast enough. As I started to leave, Dr. Brakovec, an intense young surgeon, came in. "Hi, Lenor, where are you going?" "Oh, I feel silly, Doctor . . . it's nothing, really." "I'm sure it isn't," said Dr. Brakovec, "but we'll just have a look." If Dr. Brakovec had not "looked," I would not have lived to tell this story.

Dr. Brakovec laid me out on the cold emergency room table and proceeded to check the lump. "My God, that's a hard lump. It seems to be attached to the pelvic bone. Doesn't it hurt when I tug at it? It doesn't seem to move." Nervously, I drew his attention to my left foot. "Look at the cut on my foot, Dr. Brakovec . . . couldn't the lump be a glandular infection?" He started cutting at the foot to see if there was pus. He scraped at my foot . . . it hurt, but I didn't care. I desperately wanted him to find a horrid infection, an infection drastic enough to cause the lymph nodes in my pelvic region to swell. Dr. Brakovec said that he couldn't find any infection. . . . That was the moment I got scared—gut scared. I never want to feel that scared again. I started to panic. I wanted to get up and run. Flee to my car, go to the store, do my grocery shopping, pick up my children, and continue the day as I would any other Saturday. But this wasn't an ordinary Saturday . . . it was a Saturday that would change my life forever. I didn't make it to the store that Saturday—or for a very long time thereafter.

About that morning in the emergency room, Dr. Brakovec said later, "The whole situation was not very clear cut. The mass really didn't feel much like anything I had ever felt before in that area. Enlarged lymph glands are common there, but it's pretty rare that they come on so rapidly, as it seemed to have done in your case. And if they are due to an infection they can be uncomfortable

7

and painful. Your lump wasn't. Another thing that was high on my list of possibilities that can occur in that area was a hernia or rupture that was protruding. That can get really hard, even though it's formed of soft things like intestines. It can be very hard—rock hard."

I asked Dr. Brakovec if cancer had been on his mind. "Cancer was not one of my primary considerations because of your age. Primarily, young people don't have cancer, and if they do, it's usually not the type that presented itself that morning. Young people get Hodgkin's or various lymph node cancers in which the lymph nodes are very soft and uncomfortable. No, cancer was not a primary consideration at all. You must had a big lump there and we didn't know what it was. We had to make a diagnosis."

After Dr. Brakovec finished scraping at the uninfected foot, he said, "I want an x-ray of your pelvis. You're not pregnant, are you?" he laughingly asked.

"I don't know but it's possible," I replied. "We've been trying, and I've been taking my temperature twice a day—from both ends!" Dr. Brakovec then said that x-rays were out. Surgery was the only alternative. He had to go in, he said, and find out just what was protruding from my pelvis.

Dr. Brakovec suggested doing the biopsy the next morning. In the meantime the nurse would administer antibiotics on the chance that the swelling might diminish. I knew enough to know that if it did go down, an infection of the gland was indicated. "But what if it doesn't go down, what would that mean?" I insisted.

"As I said before, Lenor, maybe it's a rupture or a hernia or . . . something." I didn't like "or something," I felt Dr. Brakovec was holding out on me. He knew something that he wasn't telling me. The thought shook my confidence in him and heightened my trepidation. I felt I had lost my only source of feedback—the only person who could explain the lump would not tell me what he thought. During the ensuing months I was to learn that Dr. Brakovec does not hold out on his patients. He gives his opinion straight, no matter how critical or hopeless the situation might be. His blunt truthfulness was something I learned to bank on. But I didn't know that then. I felt very much alone.

The nurse wheeled me into a private room. "Why a private room?" I thought. I must call Joseph . . . he won't believe it . . . I can just hear him . . . "Going in for surgery? For what? You were just going to the store!" The thought of telling my husband that "something" was wrong, that "something" had to be diagnosed surgically suddenly brought tears of genuine fright, gushing, pouring down my cheeks. Frantically, I tried to explain to the alarmed nurse why I was so panic-stricken. "My oldest daughter's godfather, Gigi, they just call him that, his real name is Alfred Cecchini—do you know him? He's a tomato farmer here in Tracy. He's wonderful, kind, caring, and he's dying of cancer!" At Christmas Gigi Cecchini's stomach hurt. He went in for a biopsy. His diagnosis: inoperable cancer of the liver. His prognosis: maybe two years to live. "It can't be cancer!" I screamed. "Not like Gigi's. Please dear God, don't let it be cancer."

By the time I phoned my husband I must have been hysterical, for I only remember him telling me, in no uncertain terms, to get hold of myself. Joseph has always been quiet and firm. That day I needed those very qualities. Joseph ended my hysteria abruptly over the phone with his quiet logic and firm control. By the time he came into my room at the hospital, later that day, I had calmed down. For him and because of him.

How could Joseph know that when he was summoned from the fields that bright spring morning his life would never be quite the same again?

The day progressed, slowly. The nurse had to give me some sedatives. I couldn't stop shaking. The antibiotics had no effect on the hard lump. It didn't change. It didn't move. It was still there. Dr. Brakovec visited me in my room that evening, and explained that the biopsy was scheduled for the next morning, Sunday morning. A radiologist would be present, and also a pathologist to read the frozen section.

Before going to sleep that night, I surreptitiously read the nurse's chart. I had to find out if something was being withheld from me. *Lenor Madruga. Surgery. Sun. 7 A.M. March 24. Possible Incarcerated Hernia.*

"Thank God," I thought, "I can rest easy. It is really just a hernia."

Sunday morning. I woke up scared. The nurses prepared me for surgery. I got up even more scared. I started shaking all over again. An elderly Catholic priest came by on his morning rounds. I didn't know him but I wanted him to pray for me anyway. He asked me, "When was the last time you went to confession?"

I told him, "I don't know. I don't care. I just want you to pray with me. Please pray that the lump is nothing!" He gave me communion. I couldn't swallow the host. My mouth was too dry. I felt as if I was going to choke to death on the wafer. What a joke: "Lenor Madruga chokes to death Sunday morning while taking communion."

The nurses wheeled me into surgery. Everyone was cheerful, too cheerful. Doctors, nurses, greeted me with: "Good morning, Lenor, everything's going to be fine, just fine." I wanted, desperately, to believe that when I woke up everything "was going to be fine." Dr. Brakovec proceeded with the surgery, assisted by my gynecologist,

Dr. Glover. These two men were to become intimately involved in my life from that moment on.

Joseph was waiting outside the operating room. Dr. Brakovec walked briskly out after the surgery, followed by Dr. Glover. Just before the two men reached Joseph, Dr. Glover abruptly turned and walked in the opposite direction. Terror gripped Joseph as he wondered why Dr. Glover did not wish to stay and talk to him.

Dr. Glover was shaken by what he had observed on the operating table. He was relieved not to have been the attending physician in the case. In the past, as my obstetrician, he had been the bearer only of glad tidings to my husband.

"It's a terrible thing," Dr. Glover said, "to have to tell someone his wife has cancer. It's like hitting them over the head. It's almost like death." Today he tells me that he did not expect me to live because of the tumor's location; even if it were possible to remove the tumor, he didn't think I would be able to survive the drastic physical procedure.

Dr. Brakovec went directly to Joseph. "It's bad," he said. "We had no idea. We think it's cancer, cancer of the bone."

"What's the prognosis?" Joseph hesitantly asked.

Shaking his head, Dr. Brakovec said, "Not good."

Stunned beyond description, Joseph walked to the front entrance of the hospital. He had to get some air. Much later, Joseph was to tell me that only one other time in his life had he ever felt so helpless, so powerless. Two years before, when his father died, his knees had given way.

A childhood friend of mine had also come to await the diagnosis. She was not close enough to hear what the doctor said, but as it turned out, she didn't have to. Joseph's expression told enough. "I don't remember if

Joseph cried," she said, "I only remember the old red handkerchief—you know, the one that all the farmers use—unconsciously go to his brow."

During the biopsy, Dr. Brakovec had found a large fixed and immovable mass on the left side of the pubis. "It appeared to be a combination of cartilage and a fleshy type material that cut easily," he reported. "It was well encapsulated—that is, separated from everything around it by a capsule of flesh. Because it had grown separate from what's around it, there were no blood vessels crossing it. But then, of course, it was still stuck on the bone, underneath. At this point, I knew it was some kind of bone or cartilage tumor—a chondroma, chrondrosarcoma, or osteosarcoma. I cut right into the lump and took out a sliver so the pathologist could make a diagnosis on the thing."

Later I asked him if he was concerned about the cancer spreading after he cut into the lump. "No," he explained, "because the capsule contained it. The public exaggerates the danger of this procedure. Sometimes you have to cut into a tumor to make a correct diagnosis. It is important that you not cut into cancer only if you're not going to remove what you've cut into."

When I awoke, everything was not fine. Dr. Brakovec was standing over me. Joseph was sitting in the standard hard-backed hospital chair, revealing nothing. "We don't know, Lenor," Dr. Brakovec said immediately. "We don't know what it is. We couldn't get it all."

Still dazed from the anesthesia, I asked, "What did the pathologist say?"

With professional calm, Dr. Brakovec said, "The pathologist couldn't give me a perfect diagnosis, Lenor. He indicated that it could be a possible chondrosarcoma or a chondroma."

"A chondro—chondrosarcoma? What's that?" I asked, even more confused and frightened.

"A chrondrosarcoma is cancer. And a chondroma is not cancer."

"But what's the difference, Doctor? I don't understand what you're saying to me."

Patiently, Dr. Brakovec tried to explain, "To the naked eye, and even under a microscope, the cells looked benign. But x-rays are needed to determine if there are any tiny spicules of bone in the tissue. This would mean that the bone itself is cancerous and is growing where it shouldn't. The pathologist could not determine this from the biopsy sample. You will have to be transferred to Stanford or Cal or somewhere where they can get at the thing. Benign or malignant, Lenor, the mass has got to come out."

Monday, the day after the biopsy, was a blur; nurses whispering in the halls about the awesome prognosis in Room 10; self-conscious friends visiting me, hating to face me, sensing some dreaded disease, relieved that it wasn't one of them. Journalist Michael Fessier, Jr., explained this reaction well in a recent article for *New West Magazine*: "It is exciting to witness calamity," he says. "It sharpens the senses, gives us the illusion of importance. Just as visiting a gravely ill person . . . heightens ones own senses . . . gives us the illusion of eternal health and life." This is natural. It's human. And it's frighteningly true. My friends visited me in groups. I guess they felt more secure, more comfortable in numbers. I tried to cheer them up. "Everything's going to be fine, the tumor may even be benign. They haven't gotten the diagnosis back from Stanford yet. It just has to come out gang!" As long as I didn't give in to the deep panic I felt inside and remained cheerful and positive, I felt everything would be all right.

Gigi came to see me; *he* was not self-conscious. After Christmas, with the knowledge that he had only two years to live, Gigi went through the rigors of chemotherapy. Surprisingly enough, the nuclear therapy did not sap his energy nor hinder him from growing 200 acres of tomatoes that spring. Security for Angie, his wife, more time with his grandchildren, and the desire to see, one last time, his tomatoes grow from seed to ripe, red maturity were his incentives.

That morning when Gigi came to see me he did not look sick. No one could have possibly guessed that he was terminally ill. He looked handsome, healthy with his typical farmer's tan which covers only face and arms but remains year round. He gave me a smile, a warm hand, and words of encouragement. No, Gigi was not self-conscious that morning.

The chemotherapy worked remarkably well on Gigi, for a while. It actually diminished the tumor, for a while. It gave him a sense of well-being, for a while. He was able to till the earth, make love, spend time with friends and family, for a while. He even bought a new red pick-up truck, enjoyed its newness, its sparkle, for a while. And then, the inevitable happened, the wild and rampant invasion of the cancerous cells to his other organs. Gigi died just short of the two-year prediction.

Monday night we still had not received word on the diagnosis of the tumor. After all my friends had left, Joseph and I were alone. We didn't say much. I think we both wanted to cheer each other up. But we didn't seem to know how. The nurse came in and said, "Visiting hours are over," thus ending our uncomfortable predicament. She gave me a tranquilizer. I was shaking again, uncontrollably. She wrapped me up, tightly, in sheets and blankets. In this protective shell I felt warm and safe, as if I was back in the womb . . . where no lumps existed.

As I lay quivering in my solid cocoon, I made a promise to God. I've never been one to ask something of God and promise to do something in return if he grants my prayer. I know that many people, particularly Catholics, believe in this form of religious plea bargaining. The Portuguese even have a word for it: *promessa*. Most Catholics conscientiously uphold their part of the bargain, whether their prayer is answered or not. Their faith leads them to a total acceptance of God's will.

That evening, I did make a *promessa*, or commitment, to God. I promised to feed the poor, visit the sick, do church work, do anything—if he would grant me one wish: my life.

The following morning, before I had even opened my eyes, Dr. Brakovec dashed into my room. "Lenor, wake up," he said. "Your tumor may be benign. We just got the pathologist's report back from Stanford. There's a 90 percent chance that your tumor is benign."

"Thank God," I said aloud. And to myself I thought, "Now what must I do to fulfill my *promessa*?"

The next morning x-rays were needed. It did not matter if I was pregnant. A mass was attached to my pelvis and they had to find out if any other bones were involved. Later, Dr. Brakovec brought in the x-ray findings and the radiologist's report from Mayo Clinic. "No other bones are involved," he said. "We still don't know if the tumor is benign or malignant. We do know it's a cartilaginous tumor, meaning it's composed mostly of cartilage. We also know it has to be removed, and, because of its precarious location, radical surgery is indicated."

"Radical surgery? What's that mean?" I asked in a barely audible voice.

"Your left leg, Lenor, most likely will have to be amputated. I cannot perform such an operation. Orthopedic surgery is needed at a cancer hospital. Maybe the Sloan-Kettering Institute in New York or the Mayo Clinic in Minnesota. I will make all the arrangements. We mustn't waste any time. Time is now vitally important."

"Amputate my left leg?" I screamed, not comprehending anything he had said about surgery or clinics or hospitals. "But I only hurt my foot while dancing. That's all. Just fix my foot. Please don't amputate my leg!"

It is probably impossible to imagine what you would feel if you were suddenly told your leg is going to be amputated. I did not grasp what Dr. Brakovec had just said. I was in a state of total shock. I kept repeating, "Please, just fix my foot, please just fix my foot!"

Two days later, on a Thursday, I was released from the hospital. I was limping from the original cutting Dr. Brakovec had done on my foot in his futile attempt to find a reason for the ugly, protruding lump. Later, people would ask me, "Why didn't you notice the lump before, especially since it was so big?" Dr. Brakovec explained, "The lump was growing from the pelvic bone outward. Before it would protrude or become noticeable it had to grow to the size of an orange." Looking back, however, I do remember one thing. When exercising, I could never seem to stretch my left leg out to the extent that I could stretch my right leg. I recall checking my groin area but it felt normal. The lump was never tender or painful.

When I got home, our lovely old house was filled with friends, flowers, gifts, and cards expressing concern . . . or was it *uneasiness?* My mother-in-law, Annabelle, scurried about the house making potfuls of hot coffee and caring for my little ones, who had no idea of the change that was about to take place in their lives. Joseph, when around me, appeared confident that everything was going to be fine. And he went about making arrangements for

the ranch so that he could leave with me to wherever I
might have to go on a moment's notice.

Nighttime was the most miserable time for me. Why
are nights always the worst when you're sick or disturbed?
Perhaps because with everything quiet, there are no
distractions, you are alone with your thoughts and your
soul. I clung to Joseph all through the night. Joseph
usually is not much of a cuddler but he never objected
once during those long uncertain nights we shared together. I kept telling myself, "Everything is going to be
all right. I can deal with the thought of my leg being
amputated, but please, dear God, don't let it be more.
Don't let this cancer be more." I prayed for my life.

Two days later, April 1, a call came from Dr. Brakovec's
office. He wanted to see us.

We drove to the office in total silence. Only the tight,
clinging grip of our hands gave any indication of the
panic we felt inside.

Dr. Brakovec met us at the door. "Come in, I've got
some information on your destination. Our pathologist,
who received his training at the Mayo Clinic in Rochester,
Minnesota, said that the doctors back there have seen
some patients with your sort of problem. A Dr. Lowery,*
I'm told, is one of the best surgeons in the country. I called
him this morning. As it happened, their bone pathologist
had read the slides and had presented them to him only
minutes before I called."

"Did the slides read benign or malignant?" I asked.

"They read malignant chrondrosarcoma, Lenor, but a
very low-grade malignancy. Let me explain. Cancer is
rated on a scale of one to four. Grade one is the least

* At the request of the Mayo Clinic, I have used pseudonyms for all the doctors
who attended me there.

malignant and grade four is most malignant. Now, there are four stages of cancer. Stage one is localized, in a particular area. Stage two spreads to adjacent structures, stage three spreads to lymph glands and stage four spreads to distant structures such as the brain or liver. Yours is a stage one with grade one rating. Meaning you have a high probability for cure."

"Why can't you do the surgery, Dr. Brakovec?" I asked, not understanding the dismal gradings of cancer or the microscopic and x-ray readings, only fearing the possibility of leaving home and family to the uncertainty of a half-life or death.

"Well, number one, Lenor, I'm not a bone surgeon. I'm what you call a general surgeon. Your condition falls in the realm of orthopedic surgery. It's quite obvious that you will need an orthopedic surgeon such as Dr. Lowery."

"Tell me the truth, Dr. Brakovec, what will happen to me at Mayo?" I asked, wanting to know, yet not wanting to know.

"Do you want it straight, Lenor?" Dr. Brakovec asked. With great effort, I nodded my head.

"A hemipelvectomy, I'm almost certain will have to be performed at Mayo."

"A what?" I asked.

"A hemipelvectomy," Dr. Brakovec repeated. "Your tumor is attached to your pelvis. The doctors will have to remove a section of your pelvis, and unfortunately, because your left leg is hooked to your pelvis, it will have to, as it were, go along for the ride. This is *not* termed an amputation. An amputation is the severing of an extremity. The tumor is not on your limb, it's on your pelvic bone. The difference between an amputation and a hemipelvectomy is the difference between an incident and a disaster. A hemipelvectomy is a very big operation. An amputation is nothing compared to it. Any bone surgeon

18

around can do an amputation, but a hemipelvectomy is something that isn't lightly embarked upon. That's why I contacted Dr. Lowery at Mayo."

"Why can't they just go in and get the tumor, why do they have to take part of my hip and my whole leg?" I asked, incredulously.

"The femoral artery is surrounded by your tumor. If they tried to dissect the tumor, it would destroy your artery. And, of course, it would leave open the possibility of the cancer spreading." Dr. Brakovec then drew a diagram to demonstrate why the tumor jeopardized my hip and leg as well.

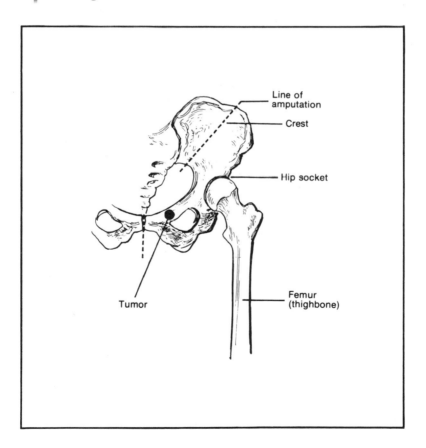

Dr. Brakovec's diagram did not register. After all, it wasn't me. It was just some physiological caricature of someone else. Not me.

"Dr. Brakovec, may I ask one more question, and please tell me the truth, am I going to die?" I blurted.

"No, Lenor, you're not going to die. I foresee a very serious and very unusual operation, but not *death*."

Joseph and I thanked Dr. Brakovec (it has always mystified me why we thank doctors, be the prognosis good or bad. If we were told we were going to die we would probably walk out the door thanking the doctor). We returned home to try to absorb this new twist of fate that had so suddenly disrupted our lives. Also, preparations had to be made for the trip East.

Dr. Brakovec watched us leave. "I felt that you were going to be cured with surgery but I didn't feel, deep down in my heart, that you fully comprehended the extent of radical surgery that I was setting up for you. You were in a state of shock. I didn't think you would ever walk again. A hemipelvectic rarely, if ever, walks. I felt you would probably be confined to a wheelchair for the rest of your life."

Last Dance

Time, you are insensitive.
When I need you most
You disappear.

Joseph and I flew to Minnesota. I felt like a seasoned jetter, for it had been only two months ago that we were on a plane flying to Mexico for our vacation where we had spent ten glorious days in Mazatlán. But now, I realized with a sinking feeling, we were not on a holiday, but on a sojourn to somewhere incomprehensible. I looked around at the other passengers. I wondered how many of them were sick? How many were headed for Mayo? Then again, maybe they were just "lucky" passengers traveling East to visit with relatives.

We had to change planes at a large modern airport in the Twin Cities for the short hop to Rochester. A young flight attendant noticed that I was limping and offered me a wheelchair.

"A wheelchair," I gasped. "No way! Please, Joseph, no wheelchair."

"Perhaps you would prefer a 'sky cap' with an electric cart," the startled young man suggested.

"What do you mean, an electric cart?" I asked.

"We have electric carts for the handicapped."

"But I'm not handicapped," I said loudly. "What makes you think I'm handicapped?"

"Excuse me, Miss, I didn't mean to infer that you were handicapped. I just thought you might need some assistance. When you got off the plane, I noticed that you were limping."

I glanced at Joseph's face and caught an expression I had never seen before—pain mixed with compassion. "Yes, thank you," I said quickly. "I could use a sky cap or electric cart . . . or whatever you call it." A sky cap and his cart were to become a necessary mode of transportation for me at every airport from that day on.

Thirty minutes later we touched down at Rochester airport. It was cold. Snow was still on the ground. As I was waiting for Joe to get our luggage, a woman I didn't recognize tapped my shoulder and said, "You must be Lenor Madruga."

"Yes, I am," I said, a bit startled.

"I'm Evie Hedstrum," she said, in a warm and friendly voice. "I live here in Rochester and my sister, Melva Wickman, who I believe is your close friend, asked me to look after you and your husband during your stay."

"Why thank you," I said. "But how in the world did you recognize me?"

"My sister told me to look for the prettiest girl and the most handsome man debarking from this flight."

It didn't take much time to realize that Evie Hedstrum

is not only efficient and kind, but also a great charmer. She is a vivacious seventy-eight-year-old widow who has devoted a great deal of her life to helping others. She has lived in Rochester for many years and knows her way around the Clinic and the hospitals. Graciously, she offers her services to the many confused and often depressed patients who arrive daily in Rochester for admittance to the famous Mayo Clinic. She picks up these utter strangers at bus stations and airports and hauls them around the city to meet their various medical appointments. Patiently, she explains the scheduling system used at the Clinic. And once they are admitted into one of the two major hospitals, St. Marys or Rochester Methodist, she offers them support and good cheer with her regular visits. Most important, however, she prays with them and for them. Evie Hedstrum is an extraordinary woman, a Christian, who became my "angel of mercy" during those three difficult weeks I spent in Rochester.

Evie drove us to our hotel in the central part of the city. To our dismay the hotel was old and cheerless. The rooms were small and cramped. The guests unnervingly appeared to be on their "last leg." In the crowded lobby of the hotel, the aged and the sick were waiting. *Waiting* to enter the large underground passageways that joined the hotel to the vast domain of the Mayo Clinic. *Waiting*, to meet their uncertain destiny.

I insisted that we change hotels immediately. After all, I wasn't old and I wasn't sick, and I didn't want to be around people who were. And those tunnels . . . they scared the hell out of me. I was not ready yet to meet my fate at the other end. . . .

We moved into the Holiday Inn a few blocks away from the Clinic. It was a typical convention-type hotel, modern, plastic, but roomy, cheerful, and alive.

The following morning Evie offered to take me to the

Clinic herself. She explained that we would probably be tied up all morning, so there was really no need for Joseph to come. She also mentioned that at Mayo tests and examinations are sometimes scheduled over a three-day period.

Evie and I arrived around nine and entered a massive reception room. We sat down with perhaps two hundred other people waiting for their names to be called. I was struck by the grandeur and immensity of the Clinic.

The Mayo Clinic is an awesome building rising nineteen stories high. On the north side of the building against a two-story-high backdrop of solid white marble, is a monumental copper sculpture of a nude male with his right arm upraised in a sign of victory. All Clinic buildings and the Methodist Hospital are connected by large underground passages.

As I sat waiting for my name to be called, a magnificent abstract mural at the end of the room caught my eye. I presumed that was its purpose—to distract the patients. I was preoccupied for only a moment, however, because my name was suddenly called out over the loudspeaker: "Lenor Madruga, would you please report to the front desk."

Evie quickly ushered me up front where I was given a booklet containing my appointments for the morning.

"Well now, that is unusual, your name being called so promptly," Evie said. It was during x-rays that I noticed a red marking on my card. It read "urgent" in bright red print. "Urgent," I thought, "that means serious. And what does red mean? Death?"

"Oh, my God, no . . . please don't let them find anything more on those x-rays," I said to myself.

While I was waiting for further tests, a woman sat down next to me outside one of the examining rooms.

She was from Wisconsin and was having x-rays taken of her hip. She told me she needed a hip replacement.

"What is a young person like yourself doing here at Mayo?" she asked.

"They think they might have to amputate my leg," I responded calmly.

Stunned, she apologized for asking. I assured her it was all right, because it didn't matter about my leg. After all, I was going to live.

"Why do they have to amputate your leg?" she wanted to know.

"Cancer," I said.

From her astonished expression, I could tell she believed me. But I could also tell she was skeptical about my chances for survival.

By the end of the morning I had had a blood test, an I.V.P. (intravenous pyelogram), and x-rays of every bone in my body.

Evie and I met Joseph for lunch. He was curious about the tests that I had taken that morning. He asked me if any were painful. Surprisingly enough, none of the tests was painful and none seemed unusual. I didn't mention, however, either to Joseph or Evie, the ominous red markings on my card.

After lunch my next appointment read *Floor 3 Room 308*. Evie had to leave us to pick up some groceries and deliver them to an elderly shut-in couple. She promised to call that evening.

No sooner had Joseph and I sat down in the large, crowded reception room than my name was called out, loud and clear, "Lenor Madruga, would you please step up to the front desk."

The nurse ushered me into a very small examining room and explained that the doctors would be in shortly.

"I'm a little confused," I said aloud, but more to myself than to the nurse. "I thought this would take a week or more before I would even see the doctor. I just arrived last night. I've only had three tests. How could they have come to a decision so soon?"

"Yes, dear," the nurse said. "It's all right. They'll explain everything. Just have a seat and relax."

I sat down but I didn't relax.

The tiny room seemed to be closing in on me. Terror began to overwhelm me, consume me. I jumped out of my chair and ran to the window, thinking, "I've got to get out of here." The streets below were icy, cold, bleak. The perfect setting—for sentencing. Which will it be, life or death?

A young doctor walked in, sat down and opened a folder on the desk. "What did your doctor say, back home, about your prognosis, Mrs. Madruga?"

"He said that I wasn't going to die," I responded quickly. "He said that you may have to amputate my leg and part of my hip but that I, definitely, was not going to die." I had to convince this young doctor that I was not going to die no matter what the new tests might have exposed. "Dr. Brakovec also said that I should be prepared for a big surgery."

"Thank you, Mrs. Madruga; is your husband here?" he asked.

"Yes. He's out in the waiting room, but why do you need him?"

"Dr. Lowery will be in directly. He wants to speak to both of you."

I felt my worst fears were coming true. Something terrible *was* going to happen to me. Why else would they ask if my husband was here? "Is this Dr. Lowery going to walk in here and tell me that the cancer has invaded other parts of my body?" I thought. "Is he going to walk in here and tell me that I am terminal with only a few months to live?"

Dizziness swept over me. A guttural sound escaped from deep within my lungs. I began to shake again. I began to pray again. . . . "Please, dear God, don't let it happen, don't let Dr. Lowery come in here and tell me something I don't want to hear, no, no, please. . . . I'm not ready!"

Dr. Lowery and Joseph walked in almost simultaneously.

Dr. Lowery was a tall, distinguished-looking man. A man who made life-and-death decisions every day for the young and old alike, a man of few words. He did not smile; his manner was almost brusque. He introduced himself and then asked me to lie down on the examining table. He checked the lump and my pelvic area.

"Mrs. Madruga," he began, "you have a chrondrosarcoma attached to your pelvis. The biopsy slide came back malignant but with a very low grade. Your tumor is called a cartilage tumor. If you must have a tumor, then it's the best one to have because it does not travel through the blood stream as most other tumors do. However, a cartilage tumor is a notorious seeder so if we try to dissect it, we run the risk of its seeding out to other areas of your body. We must perform a hemipelvectomy. Part of your pelvis bone will be disconnected from your hip and your left leg will go also. The tumor appears to have been growing in that area for maybe two years. It's a hell of a note to have to tell an attractive woman such as yourself, especially with a career in modeling, but I think you might be the type of individual that can handle it."

"Then I'm not going to die, you're going to cure me?" I asked, unbelieving.

"We feel your prognosis is very good," Dr. Lowery answered, "with a ninety-nine percent chance of cure for the future."

"Why ninety-nine percent, why not one hundred?"

"Nobody has a one hundred percent chance against cancer," he said.

"Oh, thank you, Doctor, thank you dear God, take my leg, my hip . . . whatever, as long as you let me live."

I started to babble nonsensically about how I knew how I got the tumor, explaining that two years ago, exactly, I had fallen off my horse during a barrel race competition and the horse had fallen on top of me and the saddle horn gouged into my left thigh. "Is that what caused the tumor to grow, Doctor?" I asked.

"If I knew the answer to that question, Mrs. Madruga, we could cure cancer."

I rambled on about my two little girls needing me; my beautiful old home that I had only enjoyed for three brief months; about how I ride horses, drive tractors, model, write a column. . . . "Just imagine, Doctor, I'll get to continue with my life . . . my beautiful life; I get a second chance!"

Dr. Lowery then asked if I would be prepared to enter St. Marys Hospital Saturday morning. Surgery would follow Monday morning.

"Yes," I said, through tears streaming down my face.

"It's all right," Dr. Lowery said, concern beginning to show in his voice. "You're going to be fine. You'll walk again, you can even be fitted for an artificial leg."

"I'm not crying because of my leg, Doctor; I'm crying because I'm not going to die!"

Dr. Lowery began to describe the operation. "We will have to bring part of your buttock around to close up the area we amputate. We will leave the crest of your hip so that the fitting of a prosthesis will be easier. Sometime after the operation, a prosthetist will come to the hospital and fit you with a bucket that will strap around your hips. It will fill out the area of your missing hip and you won't appear lopsided. Then, about three months from now, if the healing process goes well, you can be fitted with an artificial leg. You may be surprised to hear this," he added, "but most patients experience very little pain after the surgical amputation of a limb."

I gazed at him blankly, listening automatically. I didn't ask any questions. It sounded as though this bucket, prosthesis, and pain business was well worked out, but I simply couldn't grasp the significance of what he was saying. How could I possibly understand what he was trying to explain to me? I just kept thinking, "They're going to remove my leg—yes, I understand that, but *I am going to live!*"

It was just as well that my assumptions were so total, that I was in too dreamlike a state to ask questions. Had I known the full answers, I would not have been able to absorb them anyway.

Joseph and I left the Clinic. I was clinging to him and still crying.

"It's all right, Honey, it's all right," Joseph kept saying. I tried to make him understand that I was not crying about the leg but crying from sheer relief.

"Just think, Joseph, I'm not going to die, I'm not going to die. I'm going to get to see my little girls grow up and become women, you and I will grow old together. I want to go dancing, I want to see the sights of Rochester, let's pretend we're on a vacation . . . until Saturday."

We went back to our hotel and got ready to go out for dinner and dancing. As I bathed, in a tub full of steaming hot water, I suddenly realized that since my biopsy I had been completely ignoring my left leg. I had even denied it the courtesy of a shave. I no longer had the desire to

31

look at it, let alone touch it. It had not lived up to my expectations of remaining strong and secure next to its partner for the duration of my life. I had been weak. It had let a foreign thing grow large and destructive inside of it, without so much as a hint of warning. And because it had forsaken me, I convinced myself that it deserved its fate. It had already died as far as I was concerned, so it no longer needed care or attention.

As my distaste grew for my contaminated left leg, so did my obsession with the care and protection of my right leg. I found myself fanatically creaming the foot, the ankle, the knee, and the thigh. I meticulously trimmed and painted the toenails. In an effort to encourage it to carry its future load and to somehow compensate for the loss of its soon-to-be missing partner, I patted it and caressed it. I began to treat my right leg with renewed respect, renewed love—as if it were an only child.

Joseph and I danced after dinner in the restaurant atop the Holiday Inn. We held each other close. We swayed with the music as if we were one. I kept thinking, "I must remember this moment, the feel of legs intermingling; the grace, the ease, the control, the rhythm." The band played, typically, as their finale, "The Last Dance." I wondered, "Is this, indeed, my last dance?"

Friday we invited Evie out to dinner and a movie. Ironically, we picked a film in which Elizabeth Taylor played the part of a woman who thought cosmetic surgery to her face and body might be the answer to save her faltering marriage. The film included the actual surgery; the cutting, pulling and tying back of old flabby skin. I thought, "This woman chose, for superficial reasons, to have her skin cut away. I must have skin, bone, arteries, vessels cut away or face death. It isn't fair; I have no choice in the matter."

Driving home from the theatre I looked down at my

legs. Since I was a little girl I had received compliments on my legs. They were well-proportioned, with tapered calves and small ankles and feet. I was wearing a short black dress with gray sheer nylons. Joseph and Evie were talking about the movie. I was crying silently. I could not imagine me with only one leg sticking out from my pretty skirt.

After dropping Evie off, we drove back to our hotel. It had been over a week since Joseph and I had had sex. We have always enjoyed a very exciting and fulfilling sexual relationship. It would be difficult not to with Joseph—strong, virile, silent, the authentic Marlboro man. But, both of us seemed to have been stripped of any sexual desire since the biopsy and the uncertainty of the days that followed. That night we made an effort to stimulate our dormant desire. I kept thinking, as if in a dream, "This is the last time Joseph will ever make love to me with two legs. No, it can't be possible. This isn't happening to me, not to Lenor Madruga, the girl who always received attention for her beauty, her personality, her legs!"

From the time I was a chubby little kid living in California with my father, who was a prison guard, and my mother and two brothers and sister, I had always been everybody's favorite for my talkativeness. During my preschool years my nickname was "Gabby." We lived on various prison grounds throughout the state, the first one in Lancaster, a dusty little town somewhere on the edge of the Mojave desert in Southern California. The California Vocational Institution was a deserted Air Force barracks being temporarily used as a maximum security facility. I'm told that the bored housewives couldn't wait to see "little Gabby" coming around because she always had something informative to say about Mr. and Mrs. Smith's latest quarrel or the all-night drinking party that went on at Mr. and Mrs. Jones's. Apparently, discretion was of no importance to me. My own family's disagreements were always highest on my priority of good stories to relate. My Mom and Dad said they always warned me not to say anything to the neighbors about what went on in our home. But, without fail, after every argument I couldn't wait to gab to the neighbors. Even at four years old I was always seeking attention.

I continued to be the center of attention throughout grammar school and high school. I was voted cheerleader every time there was an election. I also ran for school president, and won—the first girl president that Tracy Senior Elementary School ever had.

During my senior year at Tracy High School my father was promoted and transferred to San Quentin Prison in San Rafael. Even being uprooted during that last important year of high school didn't phase me. I was a little upset at first having to leave all my friends and my prestigious position as cheerleader and Rally Commissioner. But it wasn't long before I was involved in everything at San Rafael High School.

While at San Rafael High I won the California State championship in Dramatic Interpretation for my solo presentation of a one-act play, and was also awarded a drama scholarship to San Francisco State College. It looked like an acting career lay ahead of me, but I was in no hurry.

After completing my sophomore year at State, I went to Europe with my sister and a girlfriend on a supposed three-month hitchhiking tour which turned into a two-year stay. Most of that time I spent in Rome, where I worked as an English language "dubber" in the old Steve Reeves *Hercules* films.

I returned to San Francisco and went to work for a

young independent movie producer who, unfortunately, went bankrupt after just a few months. Because I was in desperate need of a job, and nothing was available in theatre at the time, I tried my hand at nursing. After reading an ad in the *San Francisco Chronicle*, "Office Nurse for orthopedic surgeon," I decided that nursing was better than nothing. It never occurred to me to worry about the fact that I knew absolutely nothing about being a nurse. I dressed as demurely as possible in the eighth-grade graduation white high heels that matched my new white nurse's uniform, and went up to a Dr. Henning's office on the eighteenth floor of a downtown building and introduced myself to the receptionist. I told her I was there to apply for the position that had been advertised in the paper. She asked if I was a registered nurse.

"No," I responded.

"Then, of course, you have had some nurse's training."

"I'm afraid not," I said.

"Experience then," she prompted.

"No, but I've always wanted to be a nurse." As she began to negatively shake her head I quickly continued. "I studied biology and physiology at San Francisco State for two years and if I could just talk with the doctor, I'm sure that I could convince him of my ability and my willingness."

I started to work for Dr. Henning the following morning. Using my most convincing dramatic rhetoric I had deluded Dr. Henning into thinking that nursing was "my greatest ambition in life." My roommate, a real R.N., was horrified that I could trifle with something as important as nursing.

I threw myself into the role of "nurse." I memorized every bone in the body. In the x-ray room I said, "Yes, I know how to use the x-ray machine, if you will only refresh my memory."

"Yes," I said, "I know how to speak Spanish." And then after that every time a Spaniard or Mexican came into the office I said, "Dr. Henning, this person, I believe, is in acute pain."

"Where," he would ask.

"*¿Dónde?*" I would translate (using the one and only Spanish word I knew). And when the patient pointed to his leg, I would say, "In the leg, Doctor."

Thankfully for me and for Dr. Henning's patients, after two weeks of playing "nurse" I got a call from the new Hyatt Music Theatre. They wanted me to come and work for them. I thanked Dr. Henning for giving me the job, explaining, in a touching voice, that theatre was, actually, my greatest ambition in life.

The very next day I went to work for the Hyatt Music Theatre that had just recently been completed and was already in furious competition with the new Circle Star Theatre down the road. To my disappointment, I was put in the box office selling tickets. Within two months' time, however, I was promoted to Assistant Sales Director.

What I enjoyed most about my prestigious position was being able to meet the celebrities who performed at the theatre and to escort the local critics on opening nights. After a good six months' time playing at being an Assistant Sales Director I married my childhood sweetheart.

Joseph is the son of a Portuguese farmer who had emigrated to California and started a dairy farm. He began to drive a tractor on his father's farm when he was five, and by the time he reached puberty, he was driving his own pickup to senior elementary school. In those days, if you lived in the country and worked, you could get a driver's license when you were fourteen. Joseph went through high school during the late 1950s—picking up girls, drag racing down dark country roads, drinking Thunderbird wine and 7-Up, and making a great effort to hit every Portuguese fiesta from Los Baños to Monterey during the summer months.

We girls, even though not of Portuguese descent, tried to make it to these same fiestas to dance and have a good time, but mostly to try to attract one of these good-looking, dark Portuguese boys. To us, they seemed to possess a maturity that other boys didn't have, perhaps because they had to do men's work at such early ages. They were always tan from working outside all year; they were always well muscled from bucking hay every summer, their hair was always luxuriant, dark and wavy. They also owned the "toughest" cars in town. The fathers used to buy them almost any kind of car they wanted because the sons worked hard for them and never received wages until the time they got married. A new car might just keep them on the ranch a little longer. The Portuguese sons could do almost anything they wanted to—raise hell, drink, carouse—as long as they didn't involve their fathers in whatever they did after work; as long as they were up by 5 A.M. the next morning; as long as they didn't marry out of their nationality.

Joseph and I dated in high school over our parents' objections—mine because Joseph wasn't one of those "clean-cut Ivy League boys," Joseph's because I wasn't Portuguese. We went to the prom together. Then I went off to college and to Europe. By the time I returned, Joseph had his own farm in Tracy and was raising row crops— sugarbeets, milo, corn, and alfalfa. Our parents were tired of objecting. We married on February 21, 1965, and I moved to the country to be a farm wife.

The moment I entered the elegant lobby of the old St. Mary's Hospital to be admitted that chilly spring morning in April, I realized that this incredible thing was, indeed, happening to me. No one could take my place. Alone, I was to face the greatest challenge of my life. The thought that I walked into the hospital on two feet and would leave on only one, was more than my mind could accept. What kind of attention could I look forward to in the future? What new role must I play?

The nurses ushered Joseph and me up to a room that overlooked a bleak courtyard. Together we sat on the high hospital bed, just holding hands, not saying much of anything. The phone rang. It was my good friend, LouAnn.

"I was petrified to call you," LouAnn recalls. "I was scared to death that you would tell me that they were going to amputate your leg. I can remember the conversation as if it was yesterday. 'Hi, LouAnn,' you answered brightly. And before I could even ask what the prognosis was you said, 'Guess what, LouAnn, they're going to amputate my leg but I'm going to live.' The strange thing was that you were the one who cheered us up, Lenor; we could be calling to cheer you up, but it always ended up the other way around."

I was trying desperately to get across to my friends and family the positive fact that I was going to live. I tried to explain that, in comparison to my life, this left leg was expendable. I wanted their good cheer; I wanted their blessing, not their pity. I wanted them to be glad that I was going to live, not sad because my leg was going to be amputated. Yet for my friends, my leg always took precedence over my life. One friend explained it this way:

"We never considered the possibility of you losing your life. That just couldn't happen. But losing a leg, a disfigurement, my God, these things just don't happen to vivacious, pretty people like you, Lenor. Awful things have a way of entering only sad, lazy, ugly people's lives, we thought. We couldn't accept a picture of Lenor Madruga with only one leg. It was crazy."

After I had finished "cheering up" LouAnn, a good-looking young doctor entered the room with a clipboard under his arm. He introduced himself and explained the necessary procedures for prepping a patient undergoing radical surgery (I had to keep reminding myself that I was the "patient"). Among other things, many enemas would be needed for the purposes of sterilization. Suddenly he asked, "Do you know how fortunate you are, Mrs. Madruga?" Before I could answer, he continued, "Your prognosis is curability. Any number of Dr. Lowery's patients would gratefully change places with you. Some people come to Mayo from all over the world as a last resort, to buy a little time. You're a lucky woman."

After the doctor left, I thought over the things he had said: "fortunate," "lucky."

My leg was going to come off, and a good part of my hip. But I was going to live. *Live*. Imagine what that word means. A chance to enjoy the seasons, the weather, to breathe in the scent of freshly harvested alfalfa, make love, enjoy the fragrance for my sweet little girls in the morning. . . So much to live for. And yet now time seemed to be closing in on me, "No, stop it," I said to myself. "Don't put your thoughts back in the abyss again. Survive, girl. Survive. Believe you will survive that surgery. Believe you can get through life on one leg."

That afternoon I made two phone calls—the two most difficult I have ever made in my life. One to my mother and one to my father. Dad's was the most difficult. He and my stepmother were traveling in Acapulco. Unbeknownst to me, moments before my call was put through, Dad had received word that his only brother had just committed suicide. Shock, confusion, disbelief took hold of him. For the first time in my life, over 2000 miles of telephone wire, I heard my father break down in tears. There was no calming him, no reassuring him that everything was going to be all right. My strong, always-in-control father had reached the point of utter desolation.

I made the second call to Santa Monica, where my mother lived alone. I had said nothing to her before now. She was completely unaware of the biopsy, or the fact that I was even in Rochester for surgery. I had not wanted to worry her unnecessarily until I, myself, knew what was going to happen.

"Darling, what an unexpected surprise," she said. "How's Joseph and the girls? And how are you, dear?"

"I'm at Mayo Clinic in Minnesota, Mom. Everything's all right. Don't worry." I then went on to explain the situation, as quickly and as lightly as possible.

After I hung up, my mother was speechless, numb. She remembers thinking, What is this? Lenor calls up and says her leg is going to be amputated. Is it a joke? No, she wouldn't joke about a thing like that. But it can't be true. My baby. My little girl who always made everyone happy. Always the center of attention. Cancer, did she say? Impossible! There has never been any cancer on either side of our family. Only my father who died at seventy-nine of old age and possible signs of cancer. "No," she said out loud, "it's just not true. Plain and simple."

She called my sister, Diane. "It's true, Mom. I have Christianna and Annabelle's taking care of Daniella. Joseph's with Lenor," Diane said, as gently as possible.

Diane is two years older than I am. She has two little girls almost exactly the same ages as mine. I had phoned Diane before leaving for Mayo, asking her to care for my oldest daughter while I was away.

Diane reacted to my condition with quiet shock and surprising calm. Diane always used to panic easily, overreacting to almost any stress situation. But she surprised us all by being a strong and helpful intermediary between me and all my excitable relatives.

Sunday, the day before surgery, the nurses moved me into another room, closer to the main nurses' station. After surgery, they said I would be on I.V.'s and oxygen, and I would have to be watched very closely.

As I was getting settled in my new room which overlooked a deserted dairy that loomed dark in the distance, the phone rang. It was my oldest brother calling from Paris. I knew Ernie had just finished writing a book. But I didn't know that he was preparing to come to New York to meet with his publisher.

"What's happenin', little sister?" Ernie asked, in a phony southern drawl.

"Oh, not much, big brother," I replied in the same accent. "What's happenin' with you?"

"Seriously, Lenor, what's going on?"

"I'm going to live, Ernie," I said. "They're going to take my leg, but I'm going to live. Do you understand? I'm happy. It's all right."

"*Fantastic*, Lenor, that's *wonderful!*" When I heard that, I broke into a smile. Ernie seemed to be the only person besides Joseph whose first reaction was joy that I going to live.

A week before, Ernie had received word that his first novel, *The Rap*, was to be published. Not only that, it had been bought by a paperback publisher and accepted by a major book club. After years of scrounging through Europe, making a meager living writing newspaper and magazine articles, some successful, some not so successful, "Dirty Ernie" had made it big in the literary world. He finally had a viable property in his hands. The coming publication of *The Rap* meant happiness and independence to him and his young wife, Chiara. Money meant that Ernie could now devote all his time to writing, without the hassles of earning a supplementary living at teaching or working on the docks. Life had suddenly turned rosy for Ernie and Chiara. That spring Ernie and Paris were one, bright, colorful, optimistic. A blunt telegram he received one afternoon suddenly chilled the enchantment of Paris. It read:

> LENOR HAS CANCER . . . STOP . . . MUST AMPUTATE LEG . . . STOP . . . UNCLE FRED COMMITTED SUICIDE WITH A BULLET TO HIS HEAD . . . STOP . . . LOVE AUNT LORETTA.

And then, as if things weren't bad enough, the Seine swallowed up one of Ernie's closest friends that same afternoon.

Ernie sent red roses with a card that read:

> SOCK IT TO 'EM, LENOR!

That evening the nurses prepared me for surgery.

Monday morning I was scheduled for surgery at 8 A.M. The nurses gave me a "happy shot" around 7 A.M. By 8 A.M. I was floating, not really caring what was going to take place. The nurse came in a second time and said that my surgery had been postponed for later that morning. By 9 A.M. the euphoric effect of the shot had worn off. I asked Joseph for a pencil and paper.

"Why?" he asked.

"I want to write my impressions of what's happening, that's all. Don't you remember, honey. I promised to write some articles for the *Tracy Press* about Mayo? Please, honey, give me a pencil and paper." I started writing, feverishly, compulsively. *"Letter from Lenor: Inside St. Marys Hospital."* When the male nurse finally came for

42

me at 10 A.M., I had finished my first article, illegible, but complete. My last paragraph was a pledge to myself—and a notice to my friends.

> People are going to react to my situation as I react to it. In other words, if I'm self-pitying, others will pity me. If I consider myself an oddity, others will think me odd. I intend to continue my life with the same enthusiasm and gaiety that I'm accustomed to. All I ask is that you don't demand I keep my legs together when I dive off the diving board this summer.

I asked Joseph to try to decipher what I had written while I was in surgery. He hugged and kissed me. "See you later," he said casually. "I'm going to get a cup of coffee."

The nurse wheeled me down into the bowels of the hospital. I was keenly alert. I kept thinking, "Oh, where is that happy shot when I need it? Oh, God, why did it have to wear off so soon?" I got the shakes. Hard, steady, uncontrollable.

Another delay. They still weren't ready for me. I was wheeled into a large dark room filled with other patients strapped to gurneys. An unforgettable, foreboding quiet lay over that room. I looked to my right, a man stared blankly at me. To my left an elderly woman managed a weak smile. All these people, waiting. Waiting, to have their lives prolonged. Waiting for some kind of radical surgery. Waiting, hoping for their lives to return back to normal.

My mind flashed back to the happy sun-filled days when Joseph and I would herd cattle up at our good friend Tony Costa's hill ranch some twenty miles from our place. Eight or nine of us would gather maybe four hundred head of cattle from their grazing pastures and coax them down to the holding corrals at the home ranch below. We

43

would separate them and then systematically castrate, vaccinate, brand, and dehorn the poor unsuspecting brutes.

That morning of April 8, I was in a holding corral. Any moment my turn would come. They would delimb me, deform me, and then put me out to pasture to fend for myself.

After what seemed an eternity, my turn came. I recognized Dr. Lowery. He greeted me with warmth and confidence. I recognized the young good-looking doctor.

The anesthesiologist had difficulty injecting my vein with the anesthetic. He couldn't find a vein large enough to take the needle, a problem I've often experienced.

"What's taking so long?" I heard Dr. Lowery ask.

"I can't find a vein large enough to inject," the anesthesiologist responded, nervously.

"Try the other arm then," Dr. Lowery said, in an irritated tone. "Everything's prepared. We're ready to begin. Find a vein, now!"

I began to panic, thinking, "Oh, my God, what if they don't find a vein? I will feel everything! I will feel them cutting my leg off!"

My last conscious prayer was: "Dear God, please don't let me feel them dismembering me!"

The Awakening

I am a woman
Still. . . . .
Laden with unborn
What?

The actual surgery took about two and a half hours. I wondered then and my children ask me now, "Mommy, what did they do with your leg?" I never asked. After surgery Dr. Lowery came into my hospital room to talk with Joseph, who had been nervously waiting.

"Mr. Madruga," Dr. Lowery began, "your wife is now in recovery. The surgery was quite uneventful. Although major vessels were distorted by the tumor they were not invaded by it. There was absolutely no tumor spillage at any time during the operation and I'm quite sure that her chance of cure is very high. You must realize, Mr. Madruga, and I'm sure you do, that there is a lot of emotional trauma connected with this kind of operation. Not only for the patient but for all the doctors involved, as well."

Much later I asked Dr. Brakovec why some doctors would feel that way. "You must understand, Lenor," he said, "that we physicians are a healing entity. When, for example, one day we have a well and whole patient who suddenly shows up the next day with a cancerous condition, we feel terribly helpless. People seem to think that doctors become immune to this, but we don't. If a patient has cancer in the nose and we have to remove his nose, it is traumatic for us to see him walking around with two holes in his face where his nose should have been. Personally, it breaks my heart when I have to amputate a leg or an arm, because it is so visible, so mutilating. And it is painful to think of the limiting effects it will have on the patient's future lifestyle."

After spending two hours in recovery, I was wheeled back to my hospital room still attached to an intravenous feeding and oxygen apparatus. The following days, maybe two, are a blur. I remember the nurses covering my mouth with an oxygen mask or mouthpiece or whatever, and loudly commanding, "Blow out, Mrs. Madruga, that's it, now once more. . . . We can't allow any mucus to get trapped in your lungs, now blow out once more." I felt as if I was being smothered to death. I would grab at the thing, try to pull it away from my mouth. I couldn't understand why they were trying to muzzle my mouth.

"No, no, Mrs. Madruga, please just relax and blow out, it's all right." The nurse's calm and assertive voice would eventually relax me enough so that I could let go of the mouthpiece and return once again to my blessed stupor. Two days is a long time to ride the waves of oblivion. I believe that perhaps subconsciously I didn't want to wake up. Not just yet. It was still all too soon for me to face the hard reality of a missing leg.

The first thing I remember was asking Joseph to rub my foot. Grateful to be of any assistance, Joseph began to rub my right foot.

"No, Honey, my left foot, please rub it . . . it hurts so."

Confused, Joseph said, "But, Honey, you have no left foot."

"Rub it anyway," I pleaded. "Pretend I have a left foot, please just rub it." Obligingly, but feeling a bit ridiculous, Joseph began to rub the empty spot where my left foot would have been.

"That's good, Honey. Now rub the ankle. . . . Ah, that's better, much better. Now the knee . . . higher . . . ah, that's it. Thank you, Honey. Thank you."

Today the question I'm most frequently asked is, "What was your first reaction when you woke up and actually saw that your leg was gone?" My answer is always the same: When I finally regained full consciousness I did not, physically, feel that my leg was missing. My mind knew it, but my *nerve endings* did not. My leg was burning. There was a terrible sensation of boiling hot oil pouring slowly down it. The nonexistent foot, ankle, knee, and thigh were locked in cramps, as if my entire left leg had one big charley horse. That is why the rubbing was so important to me . . . to work out the constant, excruciating spasms that were attacking my leg. I could actually feel the full weight of my left leg. But it felt heavier than usual, almost like dead weight.

These "phantom pains" are a phenomenon experienced only by amputees. Over the years, medical experts have tried but have been largely unsuccessful in finding anything that might offer relief from this ungodly pain. Powerful drugs such as morphine work to a certain degree, but only in the beginning, when cut nerve endings are sensitive to their numbing powers. Later, after the pain has subsided somewhat, the morphine begins to create its own pain. Its hallucinogenic qualities soon make it difficult for the amputee to distinguish what is pain and what is addiction. His perceptions become distorted, confused, until he eventually becomes totally dependent on this drug. He wants, he needs, he demands more and more morphine, even though it no longer relieves his pain. He pops more pills, doubling, tripling his prescribed dosage. The painful sensations in his nerve endings have, in fact, diminished naturally. But he is unaware of this. He has already become addicted.

Some doctors feel that phantom pain is purely psychological. Its very name suggests delusion or apparition. Amputees say otherwise. Amputees know it as a very real and definite physical pain. In my own case, believe me, it was no illusion. It was real. It was vivid. And it ran absolutely wild.

When I first awoke from the anesthesia and I glanced down to where my leg should have been and saw only the flat of the sheet, I was not shocked. I think the shock was minimized because I was having such an incredible amount of phantom pain. How could I have possibly grieved over the loss of my leg when the damn thing was hurting so much? My left leg "lay" right alongside its partner of thirty-two years, right where it ought to be. The only difference was the poor devil was on fire!

If when I awakened I had experienced absolutely no sensation in the left leg, perhaps the blow might have been greater. But I awoke to a relentless pain that attacked every single bone and muscle in my leg.

I wonder if phantom pain might be an intermediary, God's intermediary, offering a sensation powerful enough to block the psychological shock one would normally experience with the sudden loss of a limb. I called phantom pain an "ungodly pain." But maybe it's the opposite—a "Godly pain," prescribed by God, to give the amputee time to adapt to his new situation.

From the moment I returned to my room Evie was

with me, hovering, protective, like a mother hen. As she recalls it: "When you returned to your room still woozy from the anesthesia, Joseph was very still. I tried to talk to him, to comfort him, but he would just answer me with monosyllables. I could see that he was terribly worried. I suggested he go out for coffee, or a cigarette or something to eat, anything to get him away from that room. It was so trying to be there with you in that room. I think what bothered me and Joseph most was your pain. You never complained but we knew you were suffering."

Almost immediately after the operation I was put on the drug Levo-Dromoran, a narcotic as powerful as morphine, and extremely addictive. I didn't care what kind of a drug it was or how addictive it was, I needed it. Levo-Dromoran worked. It shot directly to the pain, to the severed nerve endings of my left leg. It offered relief . . . in the beginning. It was given one pill every four hours. The first two hours were a breeze. But toward the latter part of the fourth hour, I needed another Levo pill desperately. The cramping, the hot oil, the extreme weight, all these sensations would start furiously attacking my leg again. The nurses were very strict about dispensing my little pill too soon. One every four hours—not one minute before. I begged, I wheedled, I cried, but no matter how dramatic I got they always stuck to the book.

"One pill every four hours, Mrs. Madruga. Now you know that. Please be patient," they would say.

The last thirty minutes of the fourth hour were always unendurable. There was nothing I could do to relieve the pain. All I could do was ask Joseph or Evie to rub the nonexistent limb . . . and pray.

My rosary beads gave me great comfort. Sometimes I would hold them so tight, while praying, that they would embed themselves in my hand. I believed that the harder I prayed, the more tightly I squeezed, the better things would be. After repeating the rosary several times, the more the better, I thought, I would again thank God for answering my prayers . . . for giving me back my life. It didn't matter why He saw fit to take my leg, it only mattered that I now had my life to look forward to. The only thing I was concerned about was my *promessa*. I hadn't specifically stated what I would do in return for God's answering my prayer, curing me of cancer. I didn't want Him to retract His commitment, so I felt that I had to get busy and start fulfilling my *promessa*.

"But what is it, Dear God," I would pray, "what is it that You may wish me to do? Please guide me, show me what it is You want from me . . . and I promise I will do it."

The very last thing I would do after prayers was to ring for the night nurse. I would ask her to wrap me up, again, in my cocoon and request that she take a pillow and prop up my . . . injury? . . . the empty place on my left side? . . . I hadn't invented a word yet to describe my wound. I called it simply *it*.

A few days after surgery necrosis affected a few of my lower stitches. Dr. Lowery explained that it was nothing to worry about—the term referred to skin that has not healed properly—dead skin. If the edges of the skin have not healed, then it is necessary to cut back to healthy skin and resuture.

"You will be under local anesthetic, Lenor, nothing to worry about. And the procedure will only take a few minutes."

The following morning they wheeled me down once again to one of the twenty operating rooms. I was scared. I didn't like reliving this surgery scenario again. I didn't like riding the gurney again. I didn't like wearing the ugly white cap again. I didn't like shaking, uncontrollably, again.

But as Dr. Lowery had promised, it was over quickly and the infection was taken care of.

Joseph was the first one to insist that I look directly at the stump. At first I didn't understand what he meant by "stump."

"Stump . . . what stump . . . what are you talking about?" I asked Joseph, confused and horrified.

"Where they amputated, Honey. What's left is called a stump. Now, you know that," Joseph said as gently as possible.

I guess I knew what Joseph was saying. And I understood the meaning of the word "stump." But God, I hated it.

Wildly I searched for another word that would mean the same as "stump" without the implication of some ugly disfigurement. "Trunk?" "Remainder?" "End?" But these words seemed even harsher. There *had* to be a word that wouldn't make amputees shudder when describing their amputation.

I was afraid to look at my amputation. I was terrified that it would be grotesque.

"It's not grotesque," Joseph said as he pulled the covers back, "it's unbelievable. It almost looks like a scar from an appendectomy . . . a little wider, perhaps."

Finally I looked. My whole left hip was swollen to an outrageous size. There was a large scar extending from my hip down to my pubic area. Thankfully, there were absolutely no visible signs of mutilation of the skin or bone. It was a clean, precise cut, almost, as Joseph had said, like a scar from an appendix operation. I found I wasn't so worried about the scar. I *was* worried about the size of my hip.

"Dr. Lowery, please," I said at my next examination. "You didn't tell me that I would be left with a big fat hip as well as no leg!"

"Your hip will look the same as before," Dr. Lowery assured me. "Your left buttock is only slightly changed. It's a little flatter than before because we had to bring around part of that skin to close up the area we amputated."

"Great," Joseph joked when I gave him the information on my derrière. "No problem. You've always been half-assed anyway."

The flood of mail I received took me totally by surprise. Some days brought thirty to forty letters and cards.

Many letters began with, "You don't know me, but—." A young teenager from Tracy sent me the following letter:

Dear Lenor,

You don't know me, but somehow that just doesn't seem to matter. Before I get too far into this letter, let me tell you about myself. I am seventeen, a senior at Tracy High. I just got home on the 18th from a stay at a hospital in S.F.

When my mother told me what you were going to have done at the Mayo Clinic, I was really stunned. But, when I read your letter in the *Press* this morning, I thought, "What a Great Lady! She's really got her head together!"

Please forgive me for typing this note, but you see, right now I'm listening to Jim Croce and thinking about you and I was kind of afraid that my tears would crap the whole damn letter up.

I was at UC because I have psoriasis. I've had it since I was six. Then I developed diabetes when I was twelve, and during this last visit it was found that I have glaucoma. So, as you can see, I have a crappy body. But, when I read your letter in the paper, you don't know how ashamed I felt for all of the times I felt sorry for myself.

Sometimes I ask God WHY? But I really know it's part of the whole picture. When I think of all the super people that I've met in the hospital, it's all been worth it. . . .

You know, when you come home from the hospital, you

have an invitation to come over and we'll share a pot of coffee, and hopefully some of that beautiful acceptance and faith will rub off on me.

This whole town is praying for you, and I hope that you are praying for us. Pray that we all don't make dumb asses out of ourselves when you come back. God knows, you are so much stronger than we.

I know that you can make it. There is no doubt in my mind. Here I sit, listening to Jim Croce and crying. I never cry from physical hurt, just when I get mad and especially when I don't know who or what to get mad at.

I was also overwhelmed by a deluge of flowers and telephone calls! Evie recalls: "Every time the phone rang you would say 'Hi, oh, I'm just fine, I'm doing great.' You were very jubilant all the time, even when you were experiencing a whole lot of pain. You never complained to anyone who called. Even when the doctors asked how you felt, it was always, 'Oh, I'm feeling fine.' "

I had to remain cheerful and optimistic. I didn't want to be sick. I didn't want others to think I was sick. My gowns had to be delicate, feminine, and in the pastel colors that suited me best. My hair had to be washed and set daily. I perspired heavily, probably because of the medication, and would insist on changing my gowns all the time. "How do I look, Evie?" I'd ask constantly. My make-up had to be applied perfectly and my smile had to be bright and exuberant. Even though, more often than not, it was forced.

To this day I still can't understand why people felt that I was so courageous. I had a tumor. It had to be removed. And to effectively remove it, they had to amputate. I was in awe that the doctors could surgically remove the beastly thing. What if it had been the type of cancer that could not have been removed surgically?

Then and since then, I've often heard remarks such

as, "She acts like nothing's happened to her; like nothing's missing."

Partly, this was my way of preventing people from pitying me. But I had also learned a lesson in acceptance that kept coming back to me. Four years ago, the young husband of a dear friend, Ann, was killed one morning on the railroad tracks in full view of her home. She and Robert were madly in love and had everything to live for. I asked Ann later how she was able to accept the premature death of her husband. I felt, at the time, that there would be no way I could live with such a tragic loss.

"What else was I to do, Lenor?" Ann said matter-of-factly. "I had to accept it. It happened and there was not a darn thing that I could do about it, so I had to accept it and live with it." What is more, Ann would never want to change places with me, and I certainly would never want to bear her burden. The loss of my husband—never. I would much rather lose my leg than my husband. Given a choice in the matter, we would always rather face our own problems than the other guy's.

I related this story to one of my nurses, Ruth, a stout, gray-haired woman with a strong, self-assured air, who surprised me one evening by remarking, "Lenor, I've been a nurse for over twenty years and I have never met a patient quite like you. It's your attitude that I don't understand. Please don't get me wrong—I think it's marvelous, it's wonderful. But I honestly cannot understand it."

I then recalled to Ruth, that only two months ago, I had read about Senator Edward Kennedy's young son having his right leg amputated because of bone cancer. "How awful!" I thought at the time. "He's probably very active and athletic—how will he ever engage in sports again?" But just last week, only a few months after his surgery, I saw a picture of him skiing at Aspen with his family. "Ruth, it is clearer than ever to me now that everyone, rich, poor, young, or old, is vulnerable to sickness, disease, accidents."

Ruth had listened to me intently, without uttering a word. Then she wrapped me up in my cocoon, propped the little pillow under my wound, and walked quietly to the door. Just before going out she turned and said with downcast eyes, "I still don't think I could accept it."

There was another memory that gave me hope. I remember my disbelief when a friend told me two years before that she was marrying a wonderful man who happened to be an amputee: he had lost his leg above the knee in a motorcycle accident. I understood when I met him. He was an Italian, dark and handsome with an outstanding physique. He walked with only a trace of a limp. But it wasn't so much his physical attributes that were so appealing, it was his personality. The way he carried himself. The way he walked into a room he seemed so self-confident! How could someone *not* be attracted to this man? It wouldn't have mattered if he had both legs missing. He had lived through a horrible accident, gone through years of hospitalization, lost a leg, and, ultimately, adjusted to his fate. He didn't feel sorry for himself. He didn't lean on others for pity. He was a man . . . a total man. That's what my friend was attracted to. And that's what I saw and admired. I wanted to project a totality too. I wanted to be totally feminine, totally sexy, and devastatingly attractive—all the things I tried to be before I had a missing leg. I didn't want people to say, "Do you remember Lenor when she used to do this or that? . . . And now, look at her, poor thing, a hopeless cripple. What a tragedy!"

My days following the operation began at 6 A.M. with the checking of my vital signs, a Levo pill for the throbbing nonexistent leg, and breakfast at 8. There was a bar over my bed so that I could hoist myself to a sitting position. Every morning Dr. Lowery would bring a group of residents in to examine my wound. They probed here and there and pronounced the incision "beautiful." They were pleased by my cheerfulness; little did they know that their probing taxed even my patience. I couldn't have dealt with them in the more difficult afternoons.

I described the burning relentless pain to Dr. Lowery. "I thought I wasn't going to have so much pain," I reminded him.

"The incision will hurt until it heals completely," he replied.

"But it's my *foot* that's hurting," I persisted. "I feel the foot."

"That will go away after a while." It never did.

Bathing was next. Then I was moved into a wheelchair and taken downstairs to physical therapy. The wheelchair ride was excruciating because I had to sit on my wound. Twice a day I made the painful trip to the therapy room where Steve, a young therapist, taught me to walk on crutches.

The main thing I wanted to learn was how to negotiate stairs. I explained to Steve that all my bedrooms were upstairs, and that getting to and from them was my first priority. The hospital also had a kitchen in which patients could learn to prepare and serve meals in a wheelchair. I refused. I was not going to cook from a wheelchair: I was going to do it on my feet, first with crutches, then with an artificial leg. I didn't even want to learn another way.

During the two weeks I was confined to St. Marys Hospital I lost 30 pounds. My normal weight had been 125 pounds. My leg weighed approximately 20 pounds, so I had lost an additional 10 pounds of total body weight.

I was now down to 95 pounds. I was warned that it would be very difficult to maintain 95 pounds, and that it would be very important to keep my weight down as low as possible for the rest of my life. It is essential for amputees to stay thin. After losing a limb the amputee has only so much body left to absorb the effects of overeating or overdrinking. The old saying, "He drank as if he had a hollow leg," is not true for the amputee. Some amputees find they are not able to drink as they used to, and get high on just a few drinks. If they continue to eat as they have in the past, the pounds will begin to add up. Once they've gained too much weight it becomes increasingly difficult to take it off. There's no "running it off" for the one-legged amputee. The remaining knee must support the entire body and one knee can only take so much stress. The heavier the amputee becomes the weaker his knee becomes, until the day it totally collapses. Learning new drinking and eating habits is the first rule for the new amputee.

The days passed quickly, but not quickly enough. I was anxious to get back home to see my little girls, my family, and friends. I know Joseph was anxious about getting back to the ranch. Our farmer friends had been watching over his fields since the day we left Tracy, even using their own men and equipment, when necessary. But Joseph felt that these men had plenty of work of their own to do and he didn't want to abuse their kindness.

A few days before I was released from the hospital a local prosthetist came to my room and measured my hips. He needed the measurements in order to make the bucket apparatus I was told about before surgery. I had completely forgotten about the thing.

The prosthetist said that the bucket would strap around my hips and would even out my left side, giving me support so I could sit and not appear lopsided. I would wear this bucket, he said, up until the time I was ready to be fitted with a prosthesis. But how could he get exact measurements of my hips when my left hip was swollen to almost double its original size? He assured me that he would make allowances for the differences when he made the bucket.

A few days before I left the hospital he came back with the bucket contraption. It was shaped in the form of my missing hip and constructed mainly of leather and foam rubber. I was still very tender and sore and it hurt when he strapped it around me. What's more, it didn't seem to fit. He told me not to worry; he thought the swelling would decrease enough in another day or two for the bucket to fit. He said I would need the bucket for the flight home, so that I could sit in an upright position.

The bucket never did fit me properly and it was so bulky that I could never wear a decent-looking dress over it. I didn't wear it home; I never did wear it.

Instead of using the bucket, I wore a tight girdle which supported my wound and eased the pain somewhat. For support on my one side, I sat on a little pillow until I was able to be fitted with a prosthesis. Even today, whenever I'm not wearing my artificial limb, I wear a tight-fitting girdle for support and tuck a little pillow under me when I sit or lie down.

Easter has always been a special day for me. But that Easter I felt that because Jesus rose from the dead long ago, I personally was given a second chance . . . at life. I felt miserable and shaky. My "leg" throbbed and burned. But I had to get to the chapel.

I put on a long cream-colored gown tied with pink satin ribbons, and a beautiful Easter bonnet that a friend had sent me. With Joseph, I crutched down the long halls that led to the chapel. People stared. Evie said I looked just as happy as if I were dressed up to go to church in my own home town. The nurses were amazed. "I will never forget the strength you displayed that Easter morning," Evie said later. "I, and everyone else, could actually feel the presence of the Lord guiding you that morning."

My true faith in God was to be tested shortly. In five days I was to journey home to face friends and family on one leg.

The Homecoming

Who do you see
When you look
ul me

Evie drove Joseph and me back to Rochester Airport for our flight home. I thought, has it only been three weeks since I last traveled this road? The snow had already melted from the ground. The road didn't seem quite as long or quite as bleak as it appeared three weeks ago. But then, a lot of things had changed.

For one thing, I was wearing a much-too-fancy long evening dress that covered everything, instead of the short dress I had worn on the trip coming out. I had spent long minutes agonizing over the choice in front of the hotel room mirror that morning. I couldn't wear my pants—my God, I wouldn't want my pant leg flapping in the wind. My daytime dresses were just too short. I was not ready to go out with an obviously missing limb. My only alternative was a three-piece long knit dress that Joseph had bought for me last Christmas. It was blue with just a hint of silver—my best color. As I was pulling on the skirt over my head to see how it would look on my altered figure, I remembered that I had worn this same dress the night Joseph and I had danced our last dance together. Tears began to well in my eyes. I brushed them quickly away, before Joseph could notice. I hadn't cried over my leg, or the pain, or anything else yet so why should I cry over our last dance? As I adjusted the skirt around my waist, I stood back and took a hard look at my image in the mirror.

"Not too bad," I said to myself, "not too bad at all. Once my hip goes down to its normal size I might even look half-way decent. No, no," I assured myself. "I will look *totally* good, as long as I stick to long dresses."

At the airport I encountered my first obstacle: how to get up the long steep stairs that led to the plane. Of course I had been practicing stair climbing with Steve, but Northwest Airlines didn't provide the short, wide stairs that my therapy classes did. The airline did provide, however, a "stair-chair," a contraption suspended on four little wheels which roll on a miniature track that carries a handicapped person up or down the ramp to the plane. After Joseph and I reluctantly said our goodbyes to our dear and loving friend, Evie, the airport attendant strapped me onto the stair-chair. And, as I continued to wave goodbye frantically to Evie, I began my slow ascent to the top of the stairs.

When I reached the plane entrance, Joseph and the stewardess were waiting for me. The stewardess handed me my crutches and directed me to the first-class section. Dr. Lowery had suggested that we fly first class because he said I would need a lot more room, and he was right. I needed a lot of room because I couldn't sit directly on my wound. No matter which way I would prop myself I would always find myself on it. How does one sit, if not on one's ass? It was ridiculous. There was absolutely no position that I could find that would not aggravate my nerve endings. Since my surgery I had been lying down most of the time. I wasn't used to sitting up for long periods. I couldn't read, I couldn't sleep, about all I could do was drink, and drink I did. Every time the stewardess asked me if I wished another glass of wine or a cocktail, I accepted. I would drink anything to help relieve this pain, sustain me until it was time for my next Levo pill.

I tried to keep my mind busy with thoughts of my children. Daniella was so little when I left, only two years old. Would she remember me? Would she still be always smiling? I couldn't wait to cuddle her in my arms again, bite her chubby little arms and legs, smell her sweet baby smell. And Christianna, my little blondie with the delicate features and quick mind. She's old enough to remember me with two legs, what would her reaction be when she sees me? I hoped she wouldn't be frightened by the sight of me . . . frightened by what's left of her mother. I quickly chided myself for that thought. "It's how you project yourself to your child, how you feel about yourself," I told myself. "That's what Christianna will notice and react to."

Joseph slept most of the trip. He is one of those people who falls asleep as soon as he buckles his seat belt on a plane. It was better that he slept during this trip. I didn't want him to be aware of the discomfort I was in. There was nothing he could do about it, anyway.

We arrived at San Francisco Airport right on time. As our big bird taxied us up to the point of disembarkation I searched for Tony and Ann among the many anticipating faces that pressed against the waiting-room windows.

"There they are, Honey, there's Tony and Ann. Let's hurry, and get off this plane." I jumped up excitedly and started to take off. Joseph grabbed me and said, "Where do you think you're going without your crutches?" I then remembered I couldn't walk off—Joseph was right, not without the aid of my crutches. And then what? "Oh, my

God," I thought, "I can't go down those steep stairs on my own, I'll have to use that chair thing again!" I began to feel panicky. Not that I was afraid to ride the stair-chair again, it was just that I didn't want Tony or Ann to see me descend from the plane in such an unseemly fashion. I was acutely aware that they had driven us to the airport only three weeks before and had watched me girlishly run up the ramp in my short dress. Now they were to witness this unbelievable scene of me being strapped to a chair and wheeled down a long ramp to the pavement below.

"No, no," I said aloud. "No, Dear, I want to go down the ramp by myself, I don't want to ride that chair."

"Don't be ridiculous, Honey, you can't do it by yourself, yet. I mean not until you're stronger." Joseph then firmly grabbed my arm and assisted me onto the chair.

As I made my slow descent down the ramp I could picture the look of shock on Tony's and Ann's faces . . . the very look I didn't want to see. For the first time since my surgery I burst out crying. I couldn't stop the tears from gushing, pouring down my cheeks. Tony and Ann came running out of the waiting room with tight smiles on their concerned faces. When they reached me they tried to hold me and kiss me saying, "It's all right, Lenor, it's all right."

I tried to explain that I wasn't crying about my leg, but because I was horrified that they should see me come off the plane strapped to a rolling chair, like a crippled or disabled person. I wanted them to know that I was the same person who left them three weeks ago, that I wasn't handicapped. But that lousy contraption belied the very image I was trying to project to them, an image of Lenor Madruga as she was when they last saw her.

"The next time," I said, gulping between sobs, "I get on or off a plane, I'll be walking. Just wait, you'll see!"

"Having known you for so many years, Lenor," Tony told me later, "I knew that you wouldn't want me to see you coming off the plane the way you did. So when Ann and I saw them strapping you into that chair thing we stood back trying to hide from you, but as I peeked around the corner and saw them rolling you down the ramp, tears came to my eyes and I cried."

An attendant with a wheelchair was waiting for me below and I got on. Ann insisted on pushing me down the long corridors that led to the airport entrance.

Joseph and Tony went to the baggage area to collect our bags and get the car. Everyone seemed to be staring at me riding in that wheelchair. I thought to myself, "They must be staring at my fancy dress or maybe I just look exceptionally attractive today. Oh, no, stop kidding yourself, Lenor . . . it's the blasted wheelchair!"

"Let's get rid of this wheelchair," I said to Ann. "I'll use my crutches instead."

"O.K., Lenor, whatever is easier, but do you know how to use them?"

"Of course, silly, what do you think I've been doing with all my time in Rochester?"

Ann pushed the wheelchair aside and then stood closely beside me. I guess she was afraid I hadn't truly adjusted to the "crutch game" yet.

Sadly, I noticed that people were still staring at me.

"Can you tell I don't have a leg, Ann, does my hip look out of proportion? Now tell me the truth!"

"I swear to God, Lenor, you can't tell you're missing anything. It almost looks as if you just hurt your leg, skiing or something and that your crutches are only temporary," Ann said.

"Oh good, then that's exactly what I will project to them all—that I hurt my leg and this is only a temporary . . . inconvenience."

Tony and Joseph drove right up to the front of the airport where Ann and I had been waiting. I hopped into the back seat with Ann. And immediately I lay back on the seat. "Oh, at last," I said aloud, "now I can stretch out and get the pressure off my stump . . . excuse me, I mean my wound. Oh, I'll think of a word yet. I hate that word 'stump,' don't you, Ann?"

Ann hesitated, then responded, "Well, it's not the gentlest word . . . but it does describe the situation now, doesn't it?"

"I guess so, but I'm going to find another word, Ann. Another word that doctors and amputees can use to describe the same situation. A new word for their dictionaries."

There was an uncomfortable silence for the next few minutes. Then Joseph said, "Hey, Ann, do you remember the black suede boots Lenor borrowed from you to take back East?"

"Yes, I remember," Ann said.

"Well, she brought only *one* back!"

There was a moment's pause and then we all broke out in relieved, welcomed laughter. Tony and Joseph then settled down comfortably to ranch talk and Ann and I caught up on the local gossip.

Ann recalls, "You were lying in the back seat turning this way and that like you were trying to find a comfortable position. You were wincing every so often. I knew that you were in pain but I didn't mention it because you weren't complaining or anything, so I figured you didn't want me to notice. After we had talked a little bit about the goings on in Tracy you asked me to rub your foot, the one that wasn't there. I couldn't believe what you were asking of me. So I sort of played along. I asked you where it was and you said it was on my lap. . . . 'Naturally, how silly of me,' I thought, 'Of course that's where it would be, right alongside your right leg that was lying on my lap.' So I began to rub that empty space. I'm not kidding, Lenor, when I started to move my hands like I was massaging your foot, the suffering left your face. It was as if I actually was rubbing your left foot. I'll never forget that drive home from the airport as long as I live."

As we turned off the freeway to familiar country roads near Tracy I began to feel very excited. I couldn't believe that in a few minutes I would hold my little daughters once again. As we approached the driveway leading up to our big old house I realized that I hadn't yet had a chance to get acquainted with my home. I hadn't even lived in it long. "Oh, well," I said to myself, "now, thank God, there will be time."

When I entered the front door and looked around at the comfortable living room with its high-coved ceilings and all the old pieces of country antiques that I had enjoyed finding and refinishing, including my favorite piece, an old oak fireplace mantel with round beveled mirror, I felt a tremendous sense of relief, that I actually had made it back home.

No sooner had I stepped into the door when I heard little footsteps running, little voices happily screaming, "Mommy, Mommy! You're home!" Annabelle had brought them both back home that day, knowing that I would want to see them the moment I arrived.

Christianna reached me first as I was still standing in the entrance. She ran for me with her arms outstretched. All too soon I realized that I would not be able to pick her up and walk with her, so I hurriedly made my way to the couch and then enfolded my little babies in my arms and held them close murmuring, "It's all right, Mommy is home now, everything's going to be fine, Mommy's home."

Christianna was the first to notice that her mommy

had something missing. "Mommy, where's your leg? Mommy, where's your other leg?" she demanded. She began to tug at my skirt, press her little palms at the empty spot. She actually lifted up my skirt and looked under frantically searching for my other leg. When she couldn't find it, she said, "Mommy, you left your leg somewhere. Go back and get it, please Mommy, go back and get your other leg!"

My heart nearly broke for my little child; she didn't understand, how could she understand . . . a Mommy with no leg!

I tried to explain that Mommy had a sick leg and the doctors had to take it so that I wouldn't get sick all over. But, I quickly added, "Mommy will get a brand new leg very soon."

Daniella was too little to comprehend any of it. She was mostly interested in my crutches and happily entertained herself with them on the floor at my foot. As the years passed, Daniella came to understand about my missing leg. It has never bothered her at all, and today she likes to curl up in "mommy's empty spot," where she feels safe and secure.

My dear mother-in-law then approached me and held me close. She kept repeating that her prayers had been answered . . . that God had returned me to my family so that her son would have a wife and her granddaughters would have a mother. She hugged Joseph, her only son, and then scurried off to the kitchen to plug in the coffeepot. She said we all looked tired and could use a cup of coffee. My kitchen became Annabelle's domain for the next year.

The four of us, Tony, Ann, Joseph and I chatted for a while—we talked about everything *but* my missing leg. I was glad. I was sick of the subject, I wanted to close it. I wanted to hear about them. I wanted to hear about our other friends, about their children, everything that had been going on since I left.

During our conversation Christianna never left my arms. She held me tight, as though she was afraid I might get away from her again. Daniella continued to play on the floor, happily engrossed with her new wooden toys.

After a while Annabelle came in with the coffee and said that I looked extremely tired and suggested that I go upstairs to bed. "Tony and Ann will understand," she said.

I was tired and I needed another pill badly. I kissed everyone goodnight and started to make my way up the stairs that led to our bedroom.

Ann recalls, "When Annabelle suggested that you go to bed, I wondered how in the world you were going to make it up the stairs. Many of your friends had talked about purchasing an elevator or an electric seat to assist you up the stairs. We had plans to have it installed on your staircase before you returned home, but there hadn't been enough time. So when you started up those stairs my heart was in my mouth. As if you were reading all of our minds you said, 'Don't worry, guys, I've been practicing going up and down stairs in therapy.' You carried one crutch on top of the other one, and with one hand on the railing, you ably moved from one step to the next. I know our heads must have been nodding with every step you took."

I knew everyone in the room was watching me go up the stairs, but it didn't seem to matter. It only mattered before, at the airport, when I had to face the initial shock of others seeing me wheeled off a plane. It upset me then, but not now, not ever again. With each step I took up the stairs I felt a deepening sense of determination to change the look of pity that I had seen on their faces earlier. So what if they see me struggle up the stairs tonight? Soon it will be easier for me and for them.

When I reached the top of the stairs, I thought, "Thank God, I can make it to my bedroom on my own. I slowly moved from one room to another, curious how they would appear to me now. I turned the light on in the girls' room first. It was how I remembered it. Large French-door windows covered the entire width of one wall with a spectacular view of my husband's fields. I had chosen a color scheme of mint green, pink, and white for my little girls' room. I had selected the bedspreads, matching flounced curtains, and the wallpaper. I had purchased the girls' twin beds and two old-fashioned dressers at a garage sale. The prettiest piece of furniture—a high-top dresser with spindled legs—had been part of my mother-in-law's wedding set.

The guest room I had decorated in black, white, and yellows. White eyelet curtains delicately criss-crossed at the tall narrow windows that offered a view of our horses and their corrals down below. An old-fashioned wicker couch and matching arm chairs completed the guest room.

As I made my way to the bathroom and turned on the light, the room nearly jumped out at me. I had forgotten how shocking the color of the tile had been. But the shock was pleasurable. The original owners of the house had covered the floor and walls in two shades of light and dark lavender tile, bordered with an intricate design of little yellow flowers with green leaves. I had selected a delicate wallpaper and placed green ferns here and there.

After refreshing my eyes with the sight of my upstairs rooms, I headed for my bedroom and went to bed. I could see the stars, through the large windows that gracefully reached up the side of my bedroom wall, and I found myself looking straight up into the black twinkling sky above, seeking God. When I was confident that I had God's attention, I thanked Him for bringing Joseph and me safely back to our home and our family. I again assured Him that I would fulfill my *promessa*. "Please," I prayed, "just tell me what it might be."

My first morning at home I awoke to the smell of fresh coffee brewing and the warm familiarity of my own bedroom. I knew, from the activity I could hear in the kitchen, that Annabelle was already downstairs preparing breakfast for the children and Joseph.

I had slept through the night without having to pop a pain pill. Maybe, I thought hopefully, the pain is easing off. The doctors did say that the pain would, eventually, go away—once the nerve endings die. However, nerve endings, I was also told, die a slow, painful death. Unfortunately, I was wrong. The worst was yet to come.

Joseph had slept lightly beside me that first night we shared our bed together, fearful that he might accidentally bump my side or hurt me in some way. He was up early and off to work before I woke up. I didn't mind. Joseph, like most farmers, was accustomed to popping in and out of the house all day. Farmers, in general, use their home as a refuge from the woes and concerns of the day. They come home for coffee, to make telephone calls, to eat, to nap, and to get out of the heat or the cold. I always enjoyed being able to stop whatever it was I might be doing and sit down with my husband and chat about what's happening on the ranch or with the children, or what I might have planned for the day. Sometimes the children and I would hop in the pickup and ride out to the fields to see the first little sugar beets break through the bare ground, to catch the milo heading out, or the corn tasseling out, or to check if the alfalfa was ready to cut. This kind of everyday togetherness brought about a closeness, a unity to our family. We developed an appreciation of what the others do with their time, their days.

I thought about Joseph's fear of accidentally kicking me. What other fears he might be harboring? Mainly, did he have any sexual fears? I wondered what our future might be, sexually. Is there a possibility that Joseph might be turned off to me now? Would lovemaking be the same as it was before? What changes would we have to make, will it feel the same, will it be the same? Before I could think about or answer any more of my own unnerving questions, I heard the unmistakable lilting voice of my friend, Marie, calling up the stairs, "Lenor, I'm coming up, are you decent?"

Marie and I held each other tight. She kept pushing the hair off my face, like a mother might do for her child. Before we had a chance to say much of anything, I heard more voices coming up the stairs. Alice came in next, and I felt a pang of envy as she laboriously came toward me. She was pregnant with her fourth child. I remembered that Alice was already pregnant when I was trying for a third pregnancy.

"Oh, how I wish things would have turned out differently for Joseph and me," I thought to myself. Joseph and I had wanted a large family—four or five children. I knew that I could still, physiologically, have more children, but it would be very difficult to carry a child with only a half a pelvis left on one side. I was told that if I became pregnant I would definitely need a wheelchair and more than likely, during the last three months of pregnancy I would be confined to bed. But I wasn't yet completely convinced that it was such a bad idea for me to have another baby. I continued for another year to entertain the possibility of another pregnancy. Seeing Alice that morning, swollen with child, on the threshold of experiencing one of the greatest joys I have ever had in life, I was damn jealous. "Dear God," I thought to myself, "if only I had found out that I was pregnant instead of finding a dumb lump on my leg."

I quickly brushed my "if it could have been" thoughts away and smiled brightly at my dear and enviable friend Alice. Other girlfriends started emerging through my bedroom door—Jenny, Gloria, and Ann. All five women were married to childhood friends of Joseph's. Their husbands were Portuguese and grew up influenced by the same ideals and customs that their fathers grew up with in Portugal. All these men have remained close friends through their adulthood. They are involved, basically, in the same industry in the same locale and have been able to keep in close touch. But I think their camaraderie goes even deeper than their mutual involvement in agriculture. It goes back to what their fathers tried to instill in them. "To be a man. To be a devout Catholic. To be conservative. To be a family man. To keep and respect your friends." Through the years we wives began to develop a warm and affectionate feeling for each other as well, assuring the continuation of our husbands' unique solidarity one step more.

We all talked at once that morning, laughing, giggling, excited. I wanted to show them all my scar so that they could see that it wasn't ugly or as grotesque as they might have imagined. I explained that my hip would soon go down to its normal size and that I would look pretty much the same as before.

Gloria recalls:

"Driving to your house that morning I wondered how I was going to act in front of you. How *does* one act with someone who has just gone through so devastating an experience? Someone you love, someone you've known all your life, someone who's always been so vivacious, athletic, glamorous, and full of B.S. I knew I didn't want to show pity that morning but I wondered how I was to avoid it. We were all very much affected by what happened to you. How could we not have been; after all, our husbands had been friends for so many years, our children were growing up together, we traveled together. Our lives were intertwined—even our hopes and our dreams. Everything had been going good for us all, and then something like this hits. What happened to you is something you usually read about in the papers, like the Kennedy boy, but it doesn't happen to a member of your own family or one of your friends. It doesn't happen so close to home.

"I tried to imagine how you were going to look now. I wondered just how much of your body was actually gone. I knew I had to control myself, I certainly wouldn't want horror to show on my face. I hoped you would set the mood for me and the other girls. If she's changed, I thought, it will change all of us. I'm glad you showed us your scar, the first thing. You wanted us to see that it wasn't horrifying. You were so proud of the clean line of the scar.

"After I left that morning I wondered how in the world you would be able to do even half of what you used to do. After seeing you with so much missing, I couldn't imagine you ever being able to ride horses again or water ski, run or dance. I didn't know how you would be able to fix dinner again for your family, much less entertain like you always did. I wondered how you were going to adapt to this new way of life. I was more worried, I think, about your mental state than I was about your physical state. I cried all the way home from your house that morning. I was crying for you and for us."

Later that morning Dr. Brakovec came over to check on me. "I was pleased with how you looked," he said.

"You were very pale, and, that in itself was a good sign. It meant that the doctors at Mayo hadn't over-transfused you. Doctors try never to transfuse a patient clear up to their pre-op level. They always try to leave the patient's blood level a unit or two short because with every unit of blood you give to the patient there's always the risk of hepatitis. The patient will naturally build up his own blood level in a couple of weeks anyway."

Dr. Brakovec then described the tests I would have to undergo in three months and every six months after that for the next five years. They would include a bone survey— x-rays of my pelvis, long bones, vertebrae, and skull. The tests were—and are—necessary to check for possible recurrence of the cancer. Psychologically, they are extremely painful. As I lie under the huge x-ray machine on the cold, steel table, I am all too aware that it will take the radiologist only one second to spot any abnormality, only one word from his lips to intimate doom.

Dr. Brakovec was not worried about future tests or how I looked that morning, he was more concerned about the amount of Levo I was taking.

"But I need them, Dr. Brakovec," I pleaded, "I mean there is no way I could get through the day without them."

"Fine, Lenor, I understand that you needed them right after the operation, but let's substitute another type of pain pill, one that isn't quite so addictive."

Dr. Brakovec prescribed Empirin with Codeine which I attempted to take in place of Levo—but not for long. The Empirin didn't touch the pain. Whenever I would feel the sharp pain returning, to begin its indiscriminate attack of my left leg, I would pop an Empirin and back it up with a Levo. I convinced myself that the more pain pills I took, the more relief I would get. It didn't work that way. The more I took, the more I wanted, thus beginning yet another, unforeseeable journey for me into the hallucinatory world of the drug addict.

After Dr. Brakovec left that morning with obvious anxiety written all over his face, I decided to take my first bath. It wasn't until the moment I attempted to get into the bathtub that I realized that I might have some difficulty. "Now let's see how this is to be done," I thought to myself, "I guess I sit down on the edge first and then swing my leg over and ease myself down." It worked.

The hot water hit my nerve endings with a welcome numbing sensation. I was to discover that either hot or cold water would always offer relief to my pain, sometimes the only means of relief.

I was already thinking about a new leg. The doctors had told me that I would have to wait maybe three months before I could even consider an artificial leg, as it ordinarily takes that long for a stump to heal, to be strong enough to support a prosthesis.

"But, I don't have a stump," I thought to myself, "I guess the doctors mean my hip must heal first."

I calculated that by August 1 I would be able to go looking for a new leg. It never entered my mind that it might be difficult because of my radical amputation for me to be fitted for a prosthesis, much less walk with an artificial limb. I was totally confident that in three months' time I would be walking again.

About 11 A.M. I was very tired, and I went directly to bed and slept until about 2 P.M. An early nap became a part of my routine for several weeks. By 2, when I would awaken, I would reach for another pain pill and take another hot bath. I then would fastidiously apply my make-up, spray perfume all over my body, select a fluffy feminine hostess gown to wear and then make my way downstairs on crutches to the living room to be with the friends who dropped by every afternoon.

During those first two weeks a deluge of family and friends descended on me bearing gifts of homemade breads, cakes, and complete dinners. They helped with the house, the yard, and the children. Some thought the constant run of people, coming and going, to be an imposition on us. It was not. I loved it.

These late afternoons and early evenings were fast becoming the most enjoyable part of the day for me. I loved feeling my pain ease with sprightly conversation. I loved how I could almost forget about my missing leg, get through those rough hours before I could take another pill, feel normal in the company of charming friends. I would never have survived those first difficult weeks if it had not been for my friends offering their support, their belief that I would make it.

Family and friends all observed the same things about my changed appearance. "When you first came home from the hospital you bore a distinct physical contrast from your former self. In the past you had always seemed robust, strong, tanned, full of boundless energy. But suddenly, after only three weeks of being away, you had become delicate, feminine, pale, soft. But what surprised us even more was that the pain of what you had gone through did not show on your face. We were all expecting your face to be lined with permanent markings, your eyes to be red, swollen, and black underneath from crying over the senselessness of what had happened to you. But there were no visible signs on your face of the horror you must have gone through. *We* all aged from trying to understand why this thing happened to you, and by suddenly realizing our own vulnerability."

In the mornings friends came by to help with the

various household chores. Marie recalls one morning in particular:

"You looked like maybe you hadn't slept well the night before. You looked very, very pale. Your face appeared waxen. We talked for a while. You confirmed our suspicion of a bad night. You said that you couldn't understand why the pain pills didn't seem to be helping as much as they did in the beginning. You mentioned, to our utter shock, that you had even doubled your prescribed dosage that night, but to no avail. We talked a little more, you assured us that if it wasn't for your blasted constant pain you would feel great, you said you felt more energetic with each day that passed and you further insisted that once the nerve endings died you would be free of pain, maybe in another month's time, you said. We hoped you were right. Jenny and I then made our way upstairs to see if there were beds to be made. I had short shorts on that morning, and as I walked up the stairs I could feel your eyes following me. A feeling of guilt came over me. Guilt that I, and not you, had two strong legs leading me, effortlessly, up your staircase. After Jenny and I finished making beds we left. You escorted us to the front door. We drove off, down the lane to the main road and I turned around once again. From across the field I could see that you were still standing in the doorway, pale and forlorn, looking after us. It gave me an eerie feeling that I can't explain, and I often wondered what you were thinking. I was hoping you weren't beginning to feel sorry for yourself, and then again I thought about your pain, and how it seemed to be slowly increasing instead of decreasing. I asked myself 'Why should one person have to suffer so much?' "

I remember exactly what I was thinking that morning. I was thinking "Hey girls, wait for me. Don't leave me behind. Please, dear God, don't let life pass me by!"

My girlfriends were a great comfort, but I need more than only female compassion. There was another vital part of life that I didn't want to be left out of: the admiration of the opposite sex. I believe that everyone needs this to confirm and strengthen the sexual part of one's being, and I know I depended on it both consciously and unconsciously to define the woman I was. Would men look at me with indifference now? With revulsion? The thought shook me profoundly. I needed, without having to share a man's bed, male affirmation that I was still a desirable woman. My male friends acknowledged my sexuality with words, with special looks, with their love, and with their cherished friendship. I received the same attention in the same ways, as if nothing was changed.

After two weeks of being served by family and friends, I began to feel guilty. I felt that making dinner was the wife's duty in any home, and that these generous women couldn't go on preparing dinners for me for the rest of my life. So I forced myself off the couch into the kitchen to start learning to cook on one leg. I knew that assuming the household duties, once again, would be just one more step in bringing a sense of normality back into our disrupted lives. And normality was exactly what I wanted, more than anything.

Joseph believed that his wife *could* and *would* do anything she set her mind to doing, as long as she received no pity from others and felt no pity for herself. Only days after I was home, Joseph would come in from the fields expecting things to be as they used to be; fresh coffee perking, house straightened, children clean, happy, and meals prepared. He didn't mind that my mother-in-law and friends assisted me daily on these household chores. He just wanted *me* to know that however I got it done, *I* could still do everything I used to do.

On one of those first mornings Joseph popped in for

his usual coffee break, expecting me to get it for him as I had always done in the past. I hurriedly jumped off the couch and crutched into the kitchen to pour him a fresh cup of coffee. I then attempted to carry the hot coffee over to him on crutches, the cup dangling precariously from my fingers. Joseph waited for me without moving. He acted as if he didn't see the struggle I was having or the frustration I was feeling. When I finally came to his side he took the cup, thanked me, and drank what hadn't spilled of the coffee without another word. Some of our friends who witnessed incidents like this were appalled. They felt that Joseph was being too hard on me. "After all, Lenor is on crutches, what does Joe expect of her?"

Because of my husband's normal expectations of me, today he drinks a full cup of coffee—every time.

After about two weeks of being home, Joseph and I made love. Naturally most of our family and friends were more curious and worried about this aspect of our lives than anything else. In the past, it was a joke among our friends, that if you came by in the afternoon and saw Joseph's pickup and Lenor's car out front, don't bother to stop. Many times, friends would forget the warning and pop in the back door, and yell up the stairs, "Hello, anyone home?" If they received no response, we would later find a note tacked to the refrigerator door saying, "Next time, please lock your door and post a sign 'Do Not Disturb.' "

We had an exciting, healthy, and still very romantic relationship with each other. When I was a young girl I remember hearing statements such as "After the first year of marriage you can expect the romance to go right out the window. But don't worry, it will be replaced by an even more satisfying experience, one of caring, security, stability." Thankfully, after ten years of marriage, Joseph and I still had both. We always enjoyed a newness, a freshness in our lovemaking which increased with the years instead of decreasing. Maybe it was because we both were sensitive to the wants and needs of the other, and to satisfy each other was the ultimate challenge.

That first night I leisurely bathed in bath oil, brushed my hair until it shone and let it fall down over my shoulders, donned the sexiest gown I owned, put my best side first . . . and that was that! I think women, more than men, misconceive what is beautiful to men and what is not. Women think that if you don't have a perfect physical equipment—face, breasts, legs, and fanny—then men will not be attracted to you.

In her moving book, *First You Cry*, Betty Rollin described her diminished feelings about her own sexuality after undergoing a mastectomy. She writes:

> I no longer found me attractive. I was damaged goods now and I knew it. It was enough to know that I was mutilated, a deformed person. If you feel deformed, it's hard to feel sexy. For me, anyway, feeling sexy had a lot to do with feeling beautiful, or at least whole.

I was determined not to let the surgery blemish my feelings about myself. My determination worked for me. I projected to my husband, that first night, that I was still soft, womanly, and eager for sex. How could he resist?

Another thing that enabled me to appreciate my own sexuality was to put myself in Joseph's place. What if he had lost his leg, I asked myself, "instead of me losing mine? Would I be less attracted to him?" Only, I decided, if he shrank from me, became morose, withdrawn, and considered himself unattractive. But if he projected masculinity, how could I possibly be immune to his seductiveness?

The only thing that really surprised me, the first time

we made love was that my pain abruptly stopped. I was in ecstasy in more ways than one! I couldn't understand why my leg would not hurt during sex and yet pain me the rest of the time. Perhaps it was because my brain was involuntarily captivated just as it was when I was engrossed in conversation. "Honey, do you realize that I had absolutely no pain in my leg during the whole time we made love?" I told Joseph later. "From now on, Dear, you may be requested to work overtime."

So our first time together was not some harrowing experience. On the contrary, it was a beautiful, rewarding experience. We were able to renew our marital vows "to love each other in sickness and in health," and by accepting our new situation we were also able to carry the validity of our love one step further.

Encore!

Flying, falling
Lifted, soaring—
Such exquisite risk!

Each year the Tracy Chamber of Commerce sponsors a Miss Tracy Pageant for women between the ages of eighteen and twenty-five. The winner of the contest can go on to compete in the Miss San Joaquin County contest, and, if she wins that, in the annual Miss California Pageant. In 1974 the Miss Tracy Pageant was heralded as the biggest event of the year in Tracy because the pageant was going to be coupled with two other major town events all to be presented the same evening: the naming of Mr. Tracy and the installation of Chamber officers.

I had served as hostess for the two previous pageants, and John Frerichs, the Chamber president, had kept me posted daily in Rochester on the progress of the upcoming pageant. "Just in case," he wrote, "you may want to hostess again this year."

The third week I was home, John came over to see whether I had made a decision. I was frankly anxious about John's first impression of me without a leg as I was with all my men friends. I felt that whatever my close male friends thought of my physical appearance would be the consensus of other men.

"I never looked at your legs before, Lenor," John

laughed. "I always had my eye on your boobs and your face."

I was thrilled that John still had faith in my ability to handle the show. It didn't matter to him if it was performed on one leg or two legs; the only thing that mattered was a successful presentation. My only obstacle seemed to be time. It was only one week off. I didn't know if I could do it. I was concerned about my pain, I certainly didn't want to be tormented by it up on stage in front of the whole town. I was worried about how I would look standing on stage supported only by crutches, and I was afraid that I might fall. Or that my pain would be so great, I would have to step down and let someone else take over.

John kept pressing me, "It won't be the same without you up there, Lenor. You can do it, I know you can," he urged.

John felt that if I made this first public appearance, any self-consciousness I might have felt about my body, or any doubts I might have about getting up in front of strangers again would be totally purged. He was right on both counts. After meeting with John, I realized that I not only wanted to do the pageant, but that I had to do it as well.

I began preparations immediately. I ventured out on my crutches and, for the first time since my surgery, drove to rehearsals in my own car. Driving was surprisingly easy for me. I realized immediately how fortunate I was to have had my left leg amputated instead of my right. I had always driven with only my right leg anyway, alternating between brakes and throttle with the same foot. Driving with one leg was no problem. Sitting on my wound was difficult. Thank goodness for my blessed little pillow. It cushioned the seat for me and it also allowed me to sit upright while driving. My first time out I was elated by the independence of driving a car—getting somewhere on my own, no crutches, no wheelchair.

John and his wife Judy also attended the rehearsals, assisting me, pampering me. I coached the contestants on make-up, grooming, and the correct way of walking on stage. Nothing exasperated me more than to see these ten beautiful young women—with twenty gorgeous legs—casually walking down the runway with shoulders hunched over and heads bowed low. Automatically, I would jump on the stage and make an attempt to show them just how they should walk. How does one walk with style and grace on crutches? In a fit of frustration, I would throw my crutches down and attempt to demonstrate, by swaying my hips to and fro, how to perform a model's walk. I wasn't very convincing.

"Just wait girls," I called out, "by next year I'll have a new leg and I'll be walking. Then I will show you how to walk with grace." I was right about walking again. I was wrong about ever walking again with grace or ease.

After about two hours of working with the contestants, John and Judy, sensing that the longer I stood, the worse my pain got, would insist that I go home. Surprisingly enough, when standing I had no problems with balance or equilibrium. I had problems only with pain. It seemed to me when standing that the blood would rush down to the end of my wound in a futile attempt to continue its normal course down my leg. But because those gates were closed to the surging blood, it would then, it seemed to me, try to force its way through the barrier vengefully pounding on the wound, causing excruciating pain. At this point I would excuse myself and hurry home, driving sometimes blinded by pain. I couldn't get home fast enough. Relief could be found only in the little bottles that now lined my dresser beside the bed.

I didn't know it, but up until the very morning of the pageant, my friends doubted that I would make it. Marie came over the morning of the pageant to see if she could help me with anything. I was sitting in the middle of the living room floor with typed cards bearing descriptions of the contestants scattered about everywhere.

"What day is it, Marie?" I asked. She replied that it was Saturday. "Oh, great, then I have plenty of time to get this show written. I thought the pageant was tonight."

Marie looked at me strangely. "It is tonight," she said. "It's Saturday, Lenor, and the pageant is tonight." "I got scared," Marie says. "It was the first time since you came home from Mayo that you appeared disoriented, not on top of everything. 'Oh, yes, that's right, it's tonight,' you said. 'I know, Marie, now would you mind listening to these descriptions of the contestants?'

"Then you started reading some of the cards to me and asking my opinion. They sounded terrific, and I told you so. After you finished reading the last card, you asked, 'By the way, Marie, what day is it today?'

"When I got home I went directly to the barn where I knew I would find my husband working. I described the morning to him and wondered, 'Why is Lenor pushing herself, why is she even doing that dumb pageant . . . what for? She doesn't even know what day it is.' Neither of us knew that you had already begun to use more and more pain pills."

That evening, as I prepared to get dressed, my little girls were in and out of my bedroom helping me dress. I chose a long, red and white print silk summer outfit that I had purchased some months before. The bare midriff blouse tied in front just under the bust and the matching long skirt flowed gracefully to the floor. I liked the Carmen Miranda effect.

"Ah-ha," I said excitedly to my daughters, "it fits

perfectly. You can't even tell Mommy doesn't have a leg."
I combed my hair and pulled one side back with a huge
red flower that matched the print in the gown. As I was
scrutinizing myself in the mirror I could hear the girls
squealing, "Daddy's home!"

"He'll have to hurry," I thought anxiously. "He won't
have much time to get ready as it is."

Getting somewhere on time with my husband during
the late spring and early summer months is an almost
hopeless undertaking. These months are the busiest times
of the year for a farmer. Their days and nights are
completely filled with preparing the ground and planting
the crops. Any social affair we might be invited to during
this time invariably takes second priority. More often than
not, I find myself attending these engagements alone.
After the spring and summer rush, things quiet down
while the crops grow toward maturity and the fall harvest.
Then my husband and I have a chance to do things
together again.

Joseph rushed in the back door and quickly took a
shower and dressed in an outfit with his favorite navy
blue blazer. It's always amazed me how he can at one
moment look the typical California farmer, complete with
boots, western shirt, Levis, and the popular agri-business
baseball cap atop his head, and then the next moment
affect a total suburban appearance. As usual, I thought he
looked fabulous.

We arrived just a few minutes before the pageant was
to begin. Joseph took me backstage and then seated
himself with our friends. From backstage I could see a
table and two comfortable chairs stage front. The table
was adorned with a full decanter of brandy and two
snifters. One chair was set for Stan Strain, who always
emceed the Chamber officers' installation. It wasn't difficult to distinguish to whom the other chair belonged.

Tucked securely in the corner of the chair's seat John had placed a little pillow. I silently thanked John for providing these small comforts. What John didn't know, however, was that as the evening progressed I began to pop my little Levo pill using his brandy as a kicker.

After surveying the stage I took a quick last-minute look at the audience. I had never seen the Tracy Ballroom so full. Some of the guests were there to see the Chamber installation, some to hear who was to be named Mr. Tracy, and others to support their favorite candidate for Miss Tracy. But I knew that many were there out of curiosity to see if I was really going to appear on stage that night.

My mind flew back to the last time I had made an appearance in Tracy, some two months before. The event was the naming of the Ten Best-Dressed Women in Tracy. It was planned as a publicity gimmick by the local stores and me to introduce the new spring fashions during a gala evening that included dinner, dancing, and a fashion show. That evening as I was helping the women dress in the back room, one of the models came rushing up to me and asked if I had heard the news yet. Whenever someone starts a sentence that way, you can be prepared for bad news. It was.

"It's Roy Dellaringa," she blurted breathlessly, "he has cancer and only one year to live."

There was a series of shocked responses: "I can't believe it," "He's so young, only twenty-four," "He just got married to the pretty Mancuso girl," "My God, it can't be true."

I was jolted. "What's happening, first Gigi and now young Roy . . . is this cancer catching?"

But after a few moments, we brushed aside the dismal reality of his illness and carried on with the fashion show. We could do this because it wasn't one of us or a member of our family. It couldn't have been anyway . . . cancer always strikes someone else.

Two weeks later I was struck by that terrible demon. I remember praying, at the time, for Gigi, who had been diagnosed six months before, and for Roy, as fervently as I prayed for myself. I thought if one of us made it, then we would all three have a chance for survival. It didn't happen that way. Roy survived after undergoing a tremendous amount of cobalt and chemotherapy treatment, and I survived after radical surgery. Gigi didn't make it.

More visions of that evening flashed before my eyes. I remembered modeling; enjoying all eyes on me, enjoying my skirt flying high exposing my legs, enjoying the way I looked and felt. A sense of loss, suddenly, pierced my heart and my soul. Tonight how will I look? How will I feel? Someone yelled out, "Only two minutes to show-time!"

I began to feel nervous about crutching out on stage. I was terrified that I might trip or fall down. I could bear almost anything but fall on my face in front of the whole town of Tracy—that I couldn't bear. The image of Lenor Madruga, not quite making it up on stage, would make a lasting impression on everyone. Their pity would be absolute. To this day, for me and for most amputees, accidentally falling down in the presence of others can be the most frustrating experience imaginable. It's not a physical hurt, but emotional—usually hurt pride. "Damn it, why did I have to fall down in front of all these people." It's a hurt that cuts deep and brings immediate tears to the eyes of the victim.

The contestants and I jumped to attention with the sound of Stan Strain's voice announcing the evening's program.

"May I present a young lady with more courage than

the entire National Football League and the new World Football League combined . . . back in the swing of things . . . and we're glad to have her back, I assure you . . ."

I could hear Stan Strain's introduction clearly from backstage. I was glad of that because I wanted to pace myself on the amount of time I would need to make it up the back steps that lead to the stage.

"Famous Tracy and Banta Fashion Consultant . . . " Stan continued.

"I better go now," I thought to myself, "before he finishes with my introduction."

"O.K., girls," I announced, "this is it. Be your prettiest, be your most charming and keep on smiling, no matter what!" Someone else, innocently, added the old theatrical good wish, "Break a leg!"

"Gab columnist for the *Tracy Press* . . . "

As soon as I reached the bottom of the stairway I realized that I was in for trouble. Six steps rose steeply to the stage. There was no railing to hold on to.

"Former dubber of Italian movies . . . "

Beads of sweat began to drip off my brow. "How am I going to get up those steps without a railing? They're just too narrow."

"Star of the Mayo Clinic . . . farm wife and mother of two . . . "

The contestants were watching me and beginning to feel uneasy. I know they were probably thinking, "How do we help her? . . . If we offer to help her up the steps will she be offended?" Nobody moved.

"The fastest lip in the West . . . "

There was nothing else to do. I laid down my crutches and crawled up the steps on my hands and one knee. The red and white silk skirt was smudged in the process. It didn't matter, I was determined to make it up on stage on my own. I reached the top and sat for a moment, gathering my composure. Then I called down, "Throw my crutches up, girls; hurry!"

"Ladies and gentlemen, Mrs. Joe, Lenor, Madruga
. . ."

I quickly brushed my skirt off, wiped my brow off with the back of my hand and with a prayer and the sign of the cross, I crutched out on stage with the biggest smile I could manage.

I slowly made my way to the stage center. The audience began to applaud. Soon it was a standing ovation that lasted several minutes. Stan kissed me and the audience embraced me with their spontaneous display of warmth and love. I was stunned, momentarily, wondering why I should receive such a tribute.

A friend who was in the audience recalls: "When you came out on stage that evening the room was charged with a tremendous amount of emotional electricity. Everyone was there to see Lenor and how she would perform, how tough she really was. Today, if you were to ask any of the people who were present that evening, who had won the beauty pageant, I would venture to say that ninety-five percent of them couldn't tell you. What amazed most of us was knowing that you had hostessed the event the year before, yet after going to hell and back, you were able to return and give a flawless performance."

If I could evoke this kind of reaction from others by merely appearing on stage, seemingly oblivious to my disability, imagine what other feats I could accomplish in the future. All it would take was *courage* to ignore my condition; *courage* to live with it; and *courage* to project to others that I was not a radically handicapped person, but a woman, who suddenly found herself saddled with a small misfortune, but did not let it overburden her. I knew that if I could accept this attitude, respect would be mine, pity would be reserved for other less fortunate individuals. I believe, too, that pity from others can be as devastating as the affliction itself. And if this pity is acknowledged by the handicapped person, then the ultimate debasement is consummated—self-pity. Once a person acquires the tragic odium of self-pity he loses not only the respect of family and friends, but also his own self-respect. Any desire that he might have had to return to a normal lifestyle soon diminishes in preference for the security of the lamentable world of the handicapped. He's a loser and nobody likes a loser; only winners are applauded.

I was a winner that evening, in that I was able to force myself to make that appearance and do the show. But I was a loser in another battle that I was silently fighting . . . my pain. As the show progressed, so did my pain. I tried to shift my position in an unsuccessful effort to not sit directly on my wound. My anguish was noticeable to no one but Stan. He knew but he never mentioned it, he just made it as easy as possible for me by automatically taking over whenever necessary. Stan closed the show just when my pain seemed unendurable.

"Thanks to a lot of people we were able to put together a show like this for your enjoyment . . . "

"Hurry, Stan," I thought to myself, "I've got to get up and off my wound, I can't stand the pain any longer."

"It takes a special person with courage to do this in spite of her own personal problem," Stan continued, "without the help and assistance of Lenor Madruga, you can imagine what kind of show John Frerichs and I might have come up with . . . "

Joseph was waiting for me in the wings. He helped me down the steps. He asked me if I wanted to sit down while they prepared the ballroom for the dance that was to follow.

"No, Honey, please, let's just walk around for a while. I've been sitting too long as it is. How did I do? How did I look? Could you tell I was in pain? Now, tell me the truth, Honey!"

All Joseph said was, "You were beautiful!" and that was enough for me to know that I had succeeded.

After a while, the music began to play and people started to fill the dance floor. Too abruptly, I thought, Joseph excused himself, saying he wanted to get another drink. My eyes bore down at the floor. I didn't want people to see the heartbreak I was feeling at Joseph's obvious nervousness at not being able to dance with me.

During that first dance I tried to tear my eyes away from the floor, to look up and smile at the dancing couples as if I was enjoying myself.

"May I have this dance, Madam?" I heard someone ask behind me. Naturally, I didn't think the offer was directed at me, so I didn't even bother to turn around.

"My darling, may I have the next dance?"

Now, "my darling" is an overly sophisticated salutation that Joseph and I often use when teasing each other, so I knew that the offer to dance was coming from my gallant husband.

"Thank you, my darling," I responded, "but my feet are killing me!"

Joseph did not laugh at my refusal, nor did he accept it. With one giant sweep he had me in his arms and on the dance floor, heedless to my objections or to the attention of anyone else around us. He held me close and we began to dance, slowly at first, so I could get the feel, the balance of dancing on one leg. I couldn't believe that I was experiencing the exquisite pleasure of Joseph's body pressed against mine; that we were actually dancing together. The ease, the rhythm, the intermingling of legs, these joys, that I had thought lost forever somewhere in Minnesota, were recaptured that moment on the dance floor of the Tracy Ballroom. So completely enraptured were my husband and I that when couples stopped dancing and began to encircle us, we hardly noticed. When the band finished playing we found ourselves in the midst of thunderous applause and screams of "Encore! Encore!"

This Pain, No Name

No one to listen
No one to hear
The voice of my loneliness
The noise of my fear.

6

Later that night, as I lay in bed, I felt absolutely euphoric. I had actually emceed the Miss Tracy Pageant from beginning to end. I had actually danced on one leg! But as I lay beside my sleeping husband, my exhilaration was suddenly deflated by excruciating pain. I realized that I had antagonized my nerve endings by sitting and standing too long. "Dear God," I thought, "where is that happy medium?" I reached for an Empirin with codeine, thinking that I had probably already taken too many Levo pills that night as it was. I waited for about an hour for some relief from the Empirin . . . nothing. I backed it up with a Levo pill. All through that night I made a conscious effort to wait four hours between pills, as prescribed, but I also found it increasingly difficult to keep track of time in my blurred, drug-induced state of mind. When my pain intensified so did my need for relief. And if it meant swallowing another Empirin or Levo pill an hour or two later, then that's exactly what I would do, unmindful of Dr. Brakovec's warnings or the warnings printed on each bottle—"one pill every four hours if needed." A pattern was formed that night that led to my eventual drug abuse.

During this period of indiscriminate "pill popping" I found the nights getting longer, my pain more agonizing, and my prayers more intense. Lying next to my husband, writhing in pain, it took every ounce of willpower I had not to wake him and seek his comfort . . . or was it his sympathy I was after? I know that I wanted him to be aware of the suffering I was going through. I wanted him to know how brave I was being by not moaning or complaining. The only thing that stopped me from crying out in the night to my husband was knowing that if I gave in to this phantom pain, it would one day totally consume me. I also knew that I, alone, had to challenge and conquer it. Phantom pain is terribly lonely pain, because there's no sharing it with another. You can't say, "Oh, remember when you had your leg cut off and how much it hurt?" If one hasn't experienced phantom pain, how then does one explain it? Sometimes, in exasperation, I would bargain with it. "O.K., now, if that's as bad as you're going to get tonight, then I can take it. But, please, don't take advantage of my patience!"

By morning the pain would subside somewhat, leaving in its wake a prickling sensation running up and down my nonexistent limb. I would try to lie perfectly still, reveling in my momentary freedom from pain, because I knew that once I moved or got up, the harsh, jabbing pain would return. And when this happened depression settled over me. "But I've only just awakened," I would cry out to God. "How am I going to get through the day and yet another night?" By not giving in to it, by hopping into the bathtub for relief; dressing up, going downstairs, feeding my family, continuing the day with my normal activities, I tried to cope with this pain. I know now that if I had given in to this formidable adversary by complaining or feeling sorry for myself it would have eventually destroyed all my self-respect and buried all the respect and compassion that was once willingly offered to me by family and friends.

Much later I discovered that I was not alone in my suffering. My husband informs me that there was a silent, agonized partner lying beside me. I asked him why he chose to remain still during those endless nights and not turn to me, cuddle me, soothe me in my pain.

He said that it took a great deal of self-control not to turn to me in the night to comfort me. He said he knew that I had to get through the pain alone. He knew that he could do nothing to relieve my pain and that sympathy would have only compounded the problem. He said that he only hoped that the pain would ease, as the doctors had assured us it would, and he knew it would take time.

Sometimes during the day, frustrated by the constant pain, I would cry out, "Damn this pain! When will it leave me alone? Will it ever leave me?"

"Isn't it better today," Joseph would ask, "than it was a week ago? And isn't it better today than it was a month ago?"

I had to agree. It was less than last week and less than a month ago. But, even so, the degree of difference was minimal. What made it so intolerable was its permanence.

Four years later, Dr. Lorne Eltherington, Associate Professor of Clinical Anaesthesia at the Stanford University Medical Center, described to me the plight of chronic pain patients that I had narrowly managed to avoid.

It seems the major problem with chronic pain sufferers is that they let their pain become the central theme of their lives. Pain patients, more often than not, start out with a very simple somatic injury that through the years becomes more of an aggravation than anything else. They begin to take drugs to relieve this aggravating pain and, very soon, they find themselves taking more and more analgesics.

It doesn't take the pain patient's subconscious long to realize that in order to get drugs he must have pain. So the reward-punishment kind of conditioning occurs. He knows that to get any kind of relief he must express pain and the more pain he expresses, the more relief he will get. But often, the relief of the pain is very superficial. He begins to experience euphoria from the drug and to withdraw from society.

Then, after a short period of time, begins to use his pain to manipulate. His interpersonal relationships begin to break down because the chronic pain sufferer thinks that in order to keep spouse and friends he must constantly remind them of his pain. Soon, family members and friends alike, are unwilling to hear about this pain. They feel guilty because they can't do anything about it and so, consequently, they try to get away. Pain, then, becomes the sole motivating factor of the patient's lifestyle and the ultimate cause of the breakdown of his family and home, and, finally, his own incapacitation. The devastating problem is that even though the initial somatic damage may have been quite mild, by all standards, its combination with severe depression, anxiety and manipulation called "pain behavior" by Steinbeck of UCLA, soon modifies every act and thought of the patient's life.

I soon realized that if I was active during sieges of intense pain, it would be less noticeable. While I was feeding the children, washing dishes, or making beds, my brain, it seemed, would choose to ignore my pain. But after completing whatever it was I had been doing and sitting down to relax, I would suddenly notice my pain returning. "Why is it," I would ask myself, "that only moments ago while putting the dishes away I didn't notice it much?"

Dr. Eltherington backed up my perception.

"For the chronic pain patient the sensible thing to do is to be as active as possible even though he has pain. The more he does, even though he is suffering, the less pain he will have. If a pain patient, for example, tries to be out of bed for an hour, instead of being in bed for 16 hours, his pain won't go away, but he will be able to function at a much higher level."

No, I did not cry out to my husband during those lonely tormented nights, but I cried silently and I prayed silently. Things got desperate for me in late June. I had already lost count of the amount of pain pills I was consuming day and night. I was confused, despondent, I could not understand why my magnificent little Levo pill no longer worked its magic powers of reducing my pain. My afternoon get-togethers were beginning earlier and lasting later, and I was drinking a great deal of red wine and insisting that my friends remain later into the evening to keep me company, to postpone that time when I had to go upstairs to meet yet another agonizing, sleepless night. One friend recalls:

"As the weeks passed we all began to notice your lack of exuberance. Your eyes seemed suddenly dulled as if they were covered with a thin but transparent veil. And when we talked to you, you would be staring straight at us, but you weren't listening. It was as if your attention span was short circuited." Because my medications were narcotics, not barbiturates, alcohol mixed well with them, and seemed to complement their effects. Thus I was drawn to drinking more and more wine.

One morning, after a long night of pill popping, coupled with agonizing pain, I called the Mayo Clinic and asked for Dr. Lowery. I was told that he was out of the country, so I agreed to speak with Dr. Jergins, one of the young doctors who had assisted Dr. Lowery with my surgery.

I made an effort to explain to Dr. Jergins how my pain was worsening instead of getting better. I came clean on the fact that I didn't know how many pain pills I was taking, daily, hourly. He was astonished and said that I must cut out all pain pills except for one Levo before going to bed at night. He gave me a thorough pep talk on my possible drug addiction if I continued to take as many pain pills as I had been. The last thing he said to me was, "We got you through the surgery, Lenor, and we cured you, now you have to get through this on your own."

I couldn't follow Dr. Jergins' advice. I tried to take only one pain pill before bedtime, but after only a short period of time I needed another pain pill very much.

The next morning, in near hysteria, I called Dr. Brakovec.

"You know that I'm not what you might call a complainer or a hypochondriac," I began. "Please, Dr. Brakovec, you've got to help me. I cannot get through another night of this constant pain without some help. I take the pain pills Mayo prescribed, I take the pain pills you prescribed, I take aspirin, tranquilizers, anything I can get my hands on and nothing, nothing touches my pain. Please, Dr. Brakovec, help me—you're a doctor, you must know of something else that can relieve me of this pain. Oh, please," I sobbed uncontrollably. "Oh, please, Dr. Brakovec, help me!"

Dr. Brakovec recalls that conversation vividly: "You were already taking the strongest thing available that could be taken by mouth. Because you were already requiring more and more pain pills only a short time after your surgery, I could see that you were heading for trouble. I tried to explain that your pain was actually easing up normally, but you were unaware of it because of your drug influence. I also told you that there was no reason for you to be experiencing so much pain, your wound was healing quite well and there was nothing unusual going on inside like an infection, so you shouldn't have been experiencing the kind of discomfort you were saying you had. So I had to assume because everything was healing properly, that your increased pain was due to habituation.''

Pain thresholds vary from individual to individual, and some doctors believe that some people actually have more nerve endings than others. Thus the reactions of radical amputees differ drastically. Some feel hardly any phantom pain at all. But there is also an important psychological element. Doctors report that patients who have been told in advance that they would have a lot of pain for two or three months after the operation, that it could be relieved somewhat by drugs, but not completely, accept pain much more readily.

But I was told before my surgery that amputation usually involves very little pain. This set me up for a different psychological reaction. My natural pain threshold was probably low. The pain was greater than I had been led to expect. And this may well have awakened the subconscious fear that something was wrong, despite the doctors' reassurances. Perhaps the wound was not healing or a tumor had reappeared. To forestall these intolerable thoughts as much as to relieve the pain, I reached for my pills and felt panicky when they did not work.

After that morning conversation with Dr. Brakovec I still wasn't convinced that there was nothing more that could be done about my pain. In desperation, I tried acupuncture. Long thin needles were stuck into the base of my spine where, the doctor explained, the nerve endings that led to my left leg were located. I was told that acupuncture would not totally eliminate my phantom pain, but would help ease it. The needles were connected to a machine that sent current through them to stimulate the nerves. I tried to concentrate on the energy that was being transmitted from the machine through the needles to my back. I thought that positive thinking would aid the treatment.

That afternoon I had my first uninterrupted nap for more than a month. However, when I awoke later, my pain was still with me, and it was as coarse and cruel as before. "Damn, those needles didn't work," I said to myself. "Damn!" In frustration, I popped another pain pill.

The following morning was a turning point for me. I casually glanced out my kitchen window while preparing breakfast for my family, and to my surprise, the mountains which are usually so visible from my kitchen window, were not there. I blinked and rubbed my eyes, trying to focus more clearly. When I opened my eyes the mountains suddenly reappeared, as resplendent and distinct as ever. Then my attention was distracted from the window for a moment by my children and when I turned back to the window, the mountains were gone again.

"My God," I asked myself, "am I losing my eyesight?" I was frightened, I was confused, and I was, definitely, under the influence of my little pills.

Later that morning there was a call from Dr. Glover's office requesting that I come in to see him right away. My friend Gloria drove me over.

My concerned local pharmacist had called both Dr. Glover and Dr. Brakovec about the amount of pills I had been getting. Neither doctor knew I had been getting prescriptions from them both, and Dr. Glover was alarmed. He believed I might well have to live with some pain for the rest of my life, and if my pill needs had escalated so quickly, who knew what would happen in the future?

"I was disturbed that day, too," Dr. Glover said, "by your physical appearance. You looked sallow, your complexion was bad. Just a few weeks before you had been

vibrant, pretty, sharp as a tack, but that afternoon you
were not the same woman. Your reasoning wasn't what
it should have been, nor your outlook on different things,
your actions, even the way you talked. I thought to myself,
'Dear God, this poor girl is already a dope addict.' I knew
then that there was only one way that you were going to
get off the drugs, and that was cold turkey."

"But I hurt, Dr. Glover," I moaned when I heard him
say that.

"I hate the fact that you hurt, but I hate even more the
fact that you are becoming an addict." Dr. Glover then
spoke very harshly. "Lenor, you would be better off dying
of the cancer than becoming a drug addict. If you decide
to fight this drug habit, it will be the biggest battle of
your life. Now, you're going to need the help of your
family and friends. I want you to tell them all that you are
going to try and get off the stuff and that you will need
their moral support, you will need them to talk to you,
to massage you, to take you out, anything to keep your
mind off your pain and your pain pills. Frankly, if you
don't get off the stuff now, today, you will lose more than
what you have already lost, and that is your self-respect
and finally, your life."

I was stunned by his words. The phrase kept rever-
berating in my mind—"You would be better off dying of
cancer. . . ."

The last thing I said to Dr. Glover that afternoon was
that the Lord had helped me so far, so I was going to ask
Him to help me the rest of the way.

"I felt that you really meant what you said, that you
would try to get off the pills, but to be honest, I wasn't
at all sure that it wasn't already too late," Dr. Glover said
later. "Seldom do you find anybody who's taking as many
drugs as you were taking have enough will power, enough
courage to get off them."

Then Dr. Glover turned to Gloria and asked if she was a good friend of mine. "If you are, take her home right now and assist her in looking for every pill bottle in the house. After you search the house together, check again by yourself, just to make sure that she hasn't hidden any pills."

He warned us that if there were any pills left in the house I would, in a moment of weakness, find them and take them. I would become desperate, he said, when experiencing the agonizing symptoms of withdrawal and would take anything I could get my hands on to relieve the pain. When Gloria was satisfied, he said, that every last pill is in her hands, then she was to take them home with her and destroy them.

As we drove home, my mind was reeling and I was terrified. There was absolutely nothing I could have done to prevent the tumor from growing inside me. But I could do something about my drug habit and that was to throw the pills out.

When we got home, we followed Dr. Glover's instructions and searched every room in the house for every pill bottle that we could find. Gloria was right at my heels, putting the little bottles into her purse. After our frenzied search, she suggested that I get to bed and rest because I looked beat. After she tucked me into bed and massaged my wound, she checked the house a second time, just to make sure that I hadn't hidden any pills from her. "Later, as I drove home," Gloria recalls, "I toyed with the idea of not throwing your pills out. I know myself well enough to know that if you had called and demanded your pills back, I would have given them to you. After all, no human being is going to watch another human being suffer, especially when you care about them. I honestly thought that one day in desperation, you would call me and insist that I return your pills because I could not imagine how you were going to tolerate that pain without the aid of your pills. To my surprise, however, you never asked me for another pain pill again. I'm glad I threw those pills out that day, Lenor, and didn't keep them, because there were many times, in the months to come, that I wished I had kept those pills to give you relief from that awful pain."

My first night without a pain pill was one of the worst nights of my life. I took hot and cold baths, and I prayed fervently to God to ease my pain, to get me through the night. The clock ticked away the seconds, the minutes, the hours, and finally, the night. By morning I was drenched with a foul-smelling sweat that soaked the sheets, the pillows, my nightgown, everything. It seemed as if poisonous liquids were slowly seeping out through my pores, my liver, my kidneys. And the more these foul liquids secreted from my body, it seemed, the more I craved my pills.

Night after night for two long, onerous weeks I suffered these agonies of withdrawal. Finally my craving eased off. My pain was still with me; it was still as intense as ever. But I saw that I could better cope with it, as it were, on a one-to-one basis, with full mental capacity, unobstructed by drugs.

Now began the battle to still the pain by other means— a battle I am fighting to this day. My only direct means of relief was massaging, rubbing, or patting of my stump. My close friends and family began to offer to massage me whenever they noticed me grimacing with pain. Different areas of the hip seemed to correspond to different parts of the missing leg. Rubbing low on the wound felt as if my entire left foot was being massaged. Rubbing higher afforded relief to my nonexistent knee and thigh. The phantom pain struck the most tender areas of my left leg—the instep and ankle of my left foot were always under constant, vicious attack. Even my toes were victimized. My friends massaged me willingly, without embarrassment. They will never know how much their massages were appreciated. The close bond between us grew even stronger as they tried to relieve me of my pain by substituting their strong hands in place of my little pain pills.

My next discovery of an effective painkiller came mercifully soon. One morning, Gloria called and invited my kids and me to go swimming at her place. She said she was going to follow Dr. Glover's orders to get me out of the house.

"Great," I said. "Thanks Gloria."

It was only after hanging up the phone that I suddenly felt panic. "Swim? My God, will I be able to swim with only one leg?" I forgot to ask Dr. Lowery (in the months to come I realized there were many things I forgot to ask the good doctor). "What about a bathing suit, how do I wear one, what will I look like in a bathing suit?"

I looked through my dresser drawers and found the little black bikini that I had worn the summer before and attempted to put it on. A strange sensation overcomes me as it did then, whenever I try to put on pants of any kind. I can never seem to get used to not putting both legs into the two leg holes. Just as I finish inserting my right leg in the proper hole I try to follow with my left leg in the other hole. Suddenly, it dawns on me that there is no leg to fill the hole. Just when I think I've adjusted to the missing limb, little aggravating things like this pop up as a grim reminder that I have not, in fact, adjusted. Maybe no one ever truly does.

I crutched over to the full-length mirror on the back of Joseph's dressing-room door. I threw my crutches aside and stood, solidly balanced on my right leg, and viewed my form in the mirror. I couldn't tear my eyes away from the image in the mirror, the one-legged bikini-clad image that was I. "My figure is still good," I assured myself, "if only my missing limb was not so obvious. Maybe a one-piece bathing suit will hide the enormity of the fact." I rummaged through my dresser drawers, tears spilling here and there, and found my one-piece black bathing suit. I tried it on. "There, that's passable," I decided, except for the gaping hole on the left side of the bathing suit.

Annabelle sewed up the left leg hole while I got the children ready to go swimming. "That's better," I convinced myself. I pulled a long bathing cover-up over the suit and the girls and I drove out to Gloria's.

When we arrived, Gloria was sunning herself beside the pool and her three children were already swimming. After greeting everyone, I whipped my cover-up off, hopped to the side of the pool and dove in.

The cold water hit my nerve endings with a numbing shock, totally obliterating the pain in my nonexistent limb. I found myself easily, almost effortlessly, swimming to the other end of the pool. It felt as if my other leg was with me, kicking in unison with its partner, as before. I swam one lap, two laps; Michael, Gloria's son, joined me; three laps, four laps; Christianna tried to follow; five laps, six laps, Gloria's daughters joined in. I couldn't believe that I was actually swimming with the strength of a normal person with two legs and that I was experiencing absolutely no pain. I knew then that nothing could hold me back . . . not pain, not a missing limb, not the disfigurement, nothing! We were all laughing and crying at the same time, children and adults alike. "Dear God in heaven," I said aloud, "thank you, thank you for allowing me to swim again, and to be free of pain for a while."

As time went on, I found that swimming would always offer immediate, complete relief to my wound. I had

115

already discovered that cold baths numbed my nerve endings for a while. But after the first numbing sensation of cold bath water, the mysterious phantom pain would always slowly creep back. Now, however, the cold water, along with my vigorous swimming, brought me absolute freedom from pain.

I found, too, that the afternoon's swim was to be the first in a series of achievements that I would have the opportunity to experience for the "first" time all over again—the experiences that I had already had as a child, when first learning to swim, to ride horses; or as a teenager when first learning to dance, water ski, drive a car. But as an adult there was one advantage; my appreciation was far greater than as a child. I was appreciative, believe me, that afternoon as I raced across the pool feeling the delicious splash of water against my face; I was appreciative that my one leg was boldly kicking for two, and I was appreciative that I was swimming and playing with my daughters and Gloria's children, enjoying their youthful enthusiasm, the day, the freedom from pain, the reality of just being alive.

"When Mom said that you and the girls were coming over to swim that afternoon," young Michael, who was only ten at the time, recalls, "I asked her how you would be able to swim with only one leg. I also asked her how come *you* had to lose your leg? Of all the mothers that came over to swim, you were the only one that liked to play in the pool with us kids. You liked to race—you always challenged us at the breast stroke and the back stroke. The other women seemed more interested in getting sun tans. They didn't want to get their hair wet, either. I was really excited that you were coming over, but I was afraid you wouldn't be able to swim or play with us as before."

Gloria had a great deal of difficulty coaxing me out of

the pool as that warm, memorable summer day came to an end. My reprieve from pain was not long enough. The swimming episode opened a new door in my mind. I began to think that if I could be totally free from pain while swimming, perhaps then, other activities could offer similar relief. My fashion shows! That was one activity I missed acutely.

The day after swimming at Gloria's, I called my assistant, Charlene, who had been substituting for me during my absence, and informed her that I would hostess the following Friday.

"That's great, Lenor, but won't it be difficult," she hesitantly asked, "I mean to hostess on one leg?"

"I don't know, Charlene, but if I can model nine months pregnant, as I did two years ago, then I'm surely not going to let a little ole missing leg stop me from hostessing," I declared with much bravado. I felt that if I could project a strong, self-assured attitude, then Charlene would not, could not pity me.

Friday morning arrived. I allowed myself the entire morning to prepare myself, physically and mentally. I selected a long, low-cut pink summer dress to wear. It was important that I look exceptionally good that first day "back on the job." I didn't want to hear, "How do you feel, Lenor? Is everything all right now?" and so on. On the few occasions that I had gone out, concerned questions such as these always left me frightened and bewildered. I couldn't bear to hear the edginess that I always seemed to detect in people's voices when they inquired about my health. "I'm fine, marvelous," I would always respond with gusto. What I really wanted to say was, "I'm cured, can't you see that, and because I'm cured I feel terrific." I knew that deep down these people thought my cheerful optimism to be a brave front. Thinking, instead, that I had to wait for no recurrence of the disease for at least five years before I could safely say I was cured. Maybe, to a certain extent, my vivacity was a front, contrived to convince myself and everyone else that I was, indeed, cured of cancer. The thought that Dr. Lowery did not "get it all" hovered over me then, and for the next four years like a dark rain cloud.

That Friday morning before leaving for the hotel where the fashion show was to be held, I waited for Joseph to come in for his usual coffee break. I needed his confirmation that I looked O.K. and I wanted him to tell me that it wasn't foolish of me to think that I could hostess the fashion show on one leg.

As Joseph entered the house, I attempted a model's stance, with hands on hips, and asked, "Well, Dear, how do I look?"

"Terrific, beautiful. But isn't your dress a little too low in front?" Joseph asked, raising one disapproving eyebrow.

"No, I don't think so. I might as well show what I've got left, right, Dear?"

Joseph did not answer my question, and when I saw that he did not find it amusing, either, I hurriedly continued, "Seriously, Dear, should I go through with this or do you think I should wait until I get an artificial limb?"

Joseph said it was up to me, if I felt like hostessing then I should do it. He reminded me, however, that I should take into consideration that I really didn't know how long it would be before I could get another leg.

He was right. I didn't know, for sure, how long I would have to wait before I could go looking for an artificial leg. It could be three months, four months, or a year, depending on how soon my wound healed. With the uncertainty of not knowing how long it would be until

I could actually walk again, and realizing that I had to get my mind off my pain, I decided to go ahead and hostess on crutches. I got my things together, threw my purse over my shoulder, kissed my husband goodbye, and drove off. During the ten-minute ride to town I tried to build up my confidence, "Now remember it's an informal affair," I said to myself. "All you have to do is go up to each table, make a little casual conversation about the clothes, and move on."

I arrived just a few minutes before show time and went directly to the back of the hotel where I knew I would find the models getting ready. The girls all ran up to me and hugged me and said how good I looked, and how nice it was to have me back. I could feel their nervousness, however, as they tried to look everywhere but at my left side. My own concern about how I looked to them diminished once I found myself caught up in the hustle and bustle of the dressing room with the models in pantyhose, half slips, and bras running about exchanging shoes, zipping each other up, styling one another's hair, and finally emerging from the dressing room, leaving only the lingering scent of their mixed hair sprays and antiperspirants behind.

"This is where I belong," I thought to myself, "right in the middle of all this activity, not lying on some couch concentrating on my pain, wishing I had a pain pill, counting the minutes, the hours, totally incapacitated."

"O.K., girls," I joyfully blurted out, "let's get this show on the road. Remember if the luncheon guests are in deep conversation, don't interrupt them, just make a turn and go on to the next table. And, please, keep in mind that you have only an hour and a half to model six different outfits, so don't linger too long at each table. And keep smiling, no matter what."

The hotel coffee shop has always been a favorite stopping place for travelers passing through Tracy. That particular morning was no exception. As I made my way through the crowded coffee shop, an elderly couple stopped me and asked how I had hurt my leg.

Their question took me by surprise because of its obvious innocence. I couldn't believe that these people actually thought that I had only hurt my leg.

"Oh, well, er, I had a skiing accident—(remembering it was summer) a water skiing accident," I kidded, never imagining that they would believe me.

"We're awfully sorry, how long will you have to be on crutches?" they persisted.

"Well, ah, not long; my crutches are only temporary."

Soon I would have an artificial limb and then my crutches *would* only be needed occasionally. I reasoned to myself that a little white lie was better than shocking these poor people to death with the truth. If I had responded to their question with, "Oh, well, you see I just lost my leg and part of my hip two months ago," they would have been horrified at the enormity of it, and I would have put them and myself in a very awkward position. It was easier to minimize the situation with a little white lie. That is the policy I've maintained to this day.

The two inquisitive coffee shop patrons will never know how they helped me that day. Their naiveté enabled me to confidently, boldly crutch up to each table, and greet the guests with charm and effervescence. I was pleased with how I looked, pleased that my missing limb was not so obvious.

Now when I was asked the inevitable, "How do you feel, Lenor?" I felt that the people who asked meant no harm, but were only concerned.

Toward the end of the show when the activity had died down and I was seated, I noticed my pain returning. I had, unfortunately, forgotten to bring my little pillow to sit on, so I had to use, instead, the back of my hands for support, which only added to my discomfort. Ann saw that my pain was worsening and suggested that I go home, pointing out that Charlene could handle the rest of the show.

"Why is it," I asked Ann, "that only moments ago while talking and laughing with everyone I didn't notice my pain? And now, when I'm sitting down, the damn pain has come back to torment me. Do I have to be busy every minute in order to be free of this pain? Why is it that when I try to relax my—uh—my—uh—stump bothers me more?"

"I don't know the answer to that Lenor, but will you please answer a question for me? Why do you always hesitate when you refer to your stump?"

"Because I detest the word 'stump!' " I said abruptly.

I had to go on detesting the word "stump" for yet another four years. It was not until recently that I did discover a replacement.

The memorable event took place over lunch with some of the announcers at the radio station where I had been voicing commercials. I happened to mention my urgency to find a new word, and just as I had almost given up hope of getting any feedback, one of the men said "Why don't you call it a medically altered limb?" Other suggestions came fast after that—"modified limb," "medically modified limb," and finally a short form of modified limb—"modilimb." "That's it!" I said. "That's the word! A modified limb is exactly what my amputation is. It's not the remainder of some big old tree that has been axed down. It's what is left of my leg or my hip, and it has been medically modified. The term is not offensive, nor does it bring to mind some horrid disfiguration."

That very day I called Dr. Brakovec, excited about my new word.

"Now, Dr. Brakovec, tell me, if you had an accident victim in the emergency room who had just had his leg severed, what would you call what is left of his limb?"

He naturally answered, "A stump."

"Right," I said. "After cleaning the wound, what would you do?"

He then explained that he would trim the crushed tissue, blood vessels, veins, and arteries. Then he would pull down the nerves, trim them, and let them retract far enough away from the end of the stump to avoid future sensitivity in that area. On occasion he would have to reamputate the bone so that skin and muscle could be pulled over the end of the bone to create a pad. Finally, he would trim the skin edges and sew it up. "After you've done all these things to that stump, what do you have left?"

Before he could answer, I said, "You have a surgically modified limb, right? Not a stump. You had a stump in the beginning. But after you did all those things in surgery, it is no longer a stump, but a modified limb—a modilimb."

After a brief silence, he said, "Lenor, I think you've got something."

I have used the term ever since, and today I don't even relate to the word "stump."

By the time I drove into our driveway after the fashion show, my wound was in spasm. It seemed to be coiled in knots, churning, throbbing and, finally, convulsing in spurts of hot oil that seemed to gush down my nonexistent limb. Annabelle met me at the front door and saw the expression on my face. "Please, Mom, I need a pain pill!" I blurted, then stopped when I saw a powerless, pitiful look cross Annabelle's face. "Well," I continued, "would you mind just rubbing my hip, it hurts so." The drug craving, I realized, was still waging guerrilla warfare. I would have to be vigilant for a while longer.

Being active was essential to keeping the pain at bay during the daytime, so I began doing household chores on one leg. I had yet another month to wait before I could go searching for an artificial leg. My crutches always seemed to be in the way. I couldn't do anything with them, and yet I couldn't get around without them. I soon learned how to set my crutches aside and hop around rooms, stabilizing myself by grabbing onto things like counter tops, chairs, doors; anything that would keep me from falling.

Not being able to carry more than a few items at a time meant many agitating trips to and from the kitchen; to discard dirty ashtrays, old newspapers, or the last drops of coffee from the bottom of cups. I secured as many things as I could in my fingers and between my teeth, when gathering articles like the children's toys, dirty socks, whatever; I would put my crutches to use by pushing and piling everything together in a big heap, so that I would only have to bend once to pick things up.

The most difficult task for me to master was carrying coffee upstairs, to my office. Since I drink a lot of coffee in the morning, I had to figure a way to get more than one cup up the staircase. I solved the problem by purchasing an insulated carafe. I carried it in the same hand that held the crutch and then set the carafe on a step as far ahead of me as I could reach. With each step I took I'd move the carafe one step also.

During my slow ascent to the top I found I was able

for the first time since we had bought the house to take time out to appreciate the old dark wainscoting that creeps its way up the staircase. I was able to enjoy the diffused colors that filter through the stained glass window that brilliantly lights up the landing; and I was able to study old family photographs that lined the walls.

Making beds proved to be the easiest chore. I would simply set my crutches aside and use the bed as a leaning post, as I hopped about smoothing the sheets and coverlets. To my delight I discovered that I could do most of the household chores that I had been accustomed to doing. It just took more time, more patience, and a lot more energy.

I had to endure the relentless, fierce, and constant aggravation of phantom pain up until two years ago. After a visit to the Stanford Pain Clinic, my pain eased considerably. But the annoying vibrations are still with me today and will probably remain with me for the rest of my life.

I found out about the existence of pain clinics through Dr. Lowery who had received a letter from a former colleague and now a patient of his about my persistent phantom pain. I met Dr. Don Yamaguchi quite by chance. He is a hand surgeon and a recent cancer victim whose malignant tumor required an above-the-knee amputation.

The afternoon we met we exchanged post-mortems on our limbs. Our discussion led to phantom pain. I described the constant pain that continued to plague me day and night. He, too, had a great deal of phantom pain. And he believed me—he believed that an amputee can suffer this pain for a long time. Ironically, before he had had his leg amputated he believed that the whole phantom pain syndrome was exaggerated. Many times, after he himself would amputate the hand of a patient, he would prescribe only a mild pain medication, assuming his patient's phantom pain to be psychological and therefore not as severe as a physical pain. Since his own surgery, he now recognizes it as a physical complaint. He had even considered writing about phantom pain, hoping that, as a doctor, he would be more credible to his peers.

Unbeknownst to me, Dr. Yamaguchi wrote to Dr. Lowery about me. Dr. Lowery wrote me:

> . . . I am very disturbed by Dr. Yamaguchi's report that you are still having very troublesome phantom pain. I was surprised to hear this because in a person who is as well adjusted as you are and as highly motivated, phantom sensations are very rarely uncomfortable and only rarely a problem. I would like to help you with this if you want to write me about it

I replied immediately to Dr. Lowery, describing my pain, and asked if he thought it could be psychosomatic. He replied:

> . . . I can assure you that the phantom pain is real and in your case, at least, has no psychological component except, as with everything else it will wax and wane a bit with emotional ups and downs. You might get some relief from injecting the sciatic nerve. I wouldn't let just anybody do this. It would best be done in an organized Pain Clinic, perhaps by an anesthesiologist. After this length of time I doubt very much if it will change spontaneously . . .

I accepted Dr. Lowery's suggestion and made an appointment with Dr. Lorne Eltherington at the Stanford University Medical Center.

Pain clinics were initiated because of an ever-increasing number of patients having only one complaint—pain—incapacitating pain. The majority of patients who come to a pain clinic have had pain for six months or more. The most common complaint (80 percent of the patients) is low back pain.

Pain clinics have just recently begun to treat terminally ill patients. The traditional approach to the terminally ill was to give them large doses of drugs and then let them slide into a calm, pain-free death. Today, however, some terminally ill patients want to function at a much higher level of awareness. They are not willing to receive large doses of narcotics which would distort and diminish their level of consciousness. Pain clinics now try to help them deal with their pain—and function normally for as long as possible.

I arrived at the Stanford Pain Clinic on the morning of May 24, 1977. My complaint was "phantom limb pain." Dr. Eltherington, a very tall, friendly, casual man, examined me and then tested my pain threshold. He placed needles superficially under the skin on my modilimb (wound) to test for increases or decreases in sensitivity. There were some hypersensitive areas. He then outlined what possible treatment might be available.

He could inject the sciatic nerve with anesthetic. If the phantom limb pain were due to irritation from the severing of the sciatic nerve, blocking this nerve with a drug that stopped it from conducting impulses between the stump and brain might stop the pain.

Surgery was another alternative. The stump could be revised, or the nerves closest to the brain could be cut. But the outcome of such surgery was very unpredictable— perhaps a few months' relief, followed by return of pain.

Drugs—antidepressants combined with tranquilizers (e.g., Triavil)—could be prescribed. But the side-effects of prolonged use could include constipation, lethargy, nausea and vomiting, apathy, tolerance, and possible addiction.

I vetoed all of these suggestions. He then suggested that an electric nerve stimulator, called a transcutaneous pain stimulator, might prove helpful. This is a very small device similar to the beeper that doctors attach to their belts. It discharges electricity through wires to small electrodes placed on the painful area. The theory is that pain messages to the brain can be blocked by an electrical jolt. A dial regulates the amount of electrical stimulation. Today these nerve stimulators are being made much smaller than a package of cigarettes and built into the prostheses themselves to control phantom limb pain.

I tried this little gadget for about a week. But all my attention was focused on my modilimb because I was uncertain of the stimulator's effectiveness. I was constantly judging whether the pain had increased or decreased. I abandoned it because it offered no relief whatsoever, although I know it has helped other amputees and chronic pain sufferers.

Nevertheless after my visit with Dr. Eltherington and after discussing the alternatives available, I was able to handle the pain on my own. I stopped considering it "pain" and used the term "sensation." Whenever the "sensation" could no longer be ignored, I would focus my attention on doing something physical, trying to occupy my mind and body totally with the activity. I asked Dr. Eltherington how I was able to do this at last, when all my previous efforts to master the pain had been so difficult. "No idea," he said. "Perhaps you only needed assurance that other ways of handling the pain existed, even if you didn't actually make use of them."

Today I still get the prickling feeling that runs up and down my nonexistent limb, and once in a while, the pain will make a quick jab at my inner thigh, my knee, my ankle, my instep—as if striking out at the injustice of the mutilation of my leg.

How to Buy a Leg

Cycle of life
Circle of pain
Crown of roses
Thorns once again.

As the three-month healing period ended, I began to inquire where I might go to buy a new leg. For convenience's sake, I thought I would first check in San Francisco for some reputable prosthetic shops. I looked in the yellow pages under artificial limbs and found two shops listed. I called each one and explained to them that I was a recent hemipelvectomy and asked if they would be able to fit me with an artificial limb. They said that there should be no problem, and gave me appointments to come in the following week. Two of my friends, Sue and LouAnn, offered to accompany me.

I had absolutely no idea of what to expect. I had never even heard the word "prosthesis" until after I had lost my leg. I thought that as soon as my modilimb had healed properly I would go to San Francisco, be fitted for a leg, put it on, and walk again. Unfortunately, it didn't happen that way. It never happens that way for the amputee.

On our way to San Francisco I was filled with hopes and fantasies of what my new leg would look like. I pictured not a plastic or mechanical leg, but a leg of flesh, bone, and skin. It never occurred to me that my new leg would look like anything other than a real life-like leg— a Barbie-doll leg. I pictured an assortment of legs all lined up together on display in sizes small, medium, and large. I never thought about what an artificial leg is made up of, or how it was to be worn, or how much it weighed. In my optimistic state of mind I thought that I would just crutch into one of these places that build limbs, choose the leg that I liked best, and walk out. Incredibly enough, no one had told me anything different.

The average person knows nothing about artificial limbs, or prostheses. Amputees number less than 1 percent of the American population. Their small number must be the reason why not much is written or heard about these implements that are vitally important to the limbless. That's why it's always an abrupt and rude awakening for the amputee, who is suddenly thrown into a world of artificial mechanical apparatuses that are his only link to an independent life.

Some amputees, like me, first look in the yellow pages (under Artificial Limbs, because Prosthetics is still too new a word) and call the shops explaining their condition. They are given an appointment and assured that they can be fitted. They are excited, full of hope and anticipation. Everything's gone right so far. Their modilimb has healed up sufficiently. They feel physically strong. They are eager to look normal again, to fill the empty sleeve or pant leg, to walk again, to be independent again. Other amputees are not so excited with the prospect of having to shop for a new limb. Many of these patients are at an all-time low in their lives. They have lost a limb because of an accident, tumor, cancer, or vascular disease; they have gone through a lot of aggravation, hospitalization, and trauma. Their amputation has cost them time and money, maybe a job, possibly even a sweetheart or spouse. They know a prosthesis is going to cost them more money. They find themselves becoming increasingly apprehensive about being fitted for a limb.

Whatever their attitude, few amputees have any idea what to expect. More often than not, they were told after surgery, "Don't worry, you can be fitted anywhere with a new prosthesis. They have made marvelous advances in prosthetics, so you will have no problem, nothing to worry about!" No names, just assurances, that anyone, anywhere, could fit them. When the time comes, however, for the amputee to be fitted, he wonders where exactly are these wonderful prosthetists that can fit anyone.

As we drove the sixty miles to San Francisco, we chatted excitedly together as if we were on one of our usual shopping sprees. I was enthusiastically optimistic as we drove into fog-enshrouded San Francisco, on that bleak August morning of 1974. We drove directly to the Sunset District where my first appointment was scheduled. The shop was small but warm and inviting. I was to find out that a pleasant and attractive atmosphere is not what one can usually expect to find at the average prosthetic shop. Most of them are drab, small, and located in the worst part of town. In time, I would understand why. It really doesn't matter where these shops are located or what they look like. I, personally, would have gone to the ends of the earth to find what I wanted and needed so desperately.

The receptionist greeted us and ushered us to a back room. I was suddenly stopped short by some outrageous things that were on display in large showcases lining the hallway. Arranged with much care was an assortment of fingers, hands, arms, breasts, ears. I couldn't believe what I was seeing. We began giggling and pointing like children. "Did you see that nose?" "Look at the hand with hair on it!" It was as though we were in a department store, looking into display cases for something new to buy. The difference was that the ornaments on display here were not for fun, but were needed to fill an empty hole on one's face, to extend a severed limb so that one might hold a child or a pencil, or for the purpose of helping a person to be mobile, independent, whole again.

There was a steady sound of hammering from a back room somewhere and the smell of glue filled the room.

The prosthetist entered wearing an apron covered with sawdust. This man had been working on patients' legs, but instead of blood covering his shirt as a doctor might have had, he was covered with dust, glue, and grease. He was carrying something black, something huge, something grotesque.

"What in the world is that?" I asked even before greeting the man.

"This is an artificial leg that belongs to a rather large black lady," he said, after first introducing himself.

"But, I, uh, I don't understand," I said with my stomach suddenly turning over. "I'm a model, I need a pretty leg, a little leg; not a leg that looks like that. What is that big thing the leg is attached to, anyway, and that strap? I don't understand what you're showing me. I could never wear a contraption that looks like that, much less walk with the thing. It's not even the right color!" I gasped.

The prosthetist tried to explain, as gently as possible, that what he was showing me was the only thing available to the radical amputee. Because a hemipelvectomy has no dangling limb, he explained, a bucket is needed which straps around the patient's hips, to give the artificial limb something to attach itself to. If I had had a stump left, the prosthesis could have easily attached itself to the stump, eliminating any need for the bucket. The strap I saw was a harness, he said, which held the leg and the bucket securely in place. He demonstrated how it was to be worn by strapping it around his back and shoulders. All I could think of, at that moment, was that if I had to wear a harness like that, how would I ever be able to wear summer sun dresses or delicate evening gowns?

I could barely get the next question out. "Can't you make me another type of leg, one that's not so big and ugly? I can understand the need for the bucket, but will

I need a harness and all those metal rings and rollers that I see inside the bucket?"

He told me that he was sorry. What he was showing me was the only type of artificial limb that was available to the hemipelvectomy. Because there are so few radical amputees, he explained, there is no demand for a more sophisticated apparatus.

"I think that you should be grateful that even this is available to you, Mrs. Madruga," he said in a courteous, but irrefutable tone of voice. "You have three choices concerning how you'll get around: an artificial limb like the one I've shown you, crutches, or a wheelchair. The decision is yours."

"But there must be someone, somewhere who can build me a leg that will enable me to walk, and at the same time be a reasonable facsimile of my original leg!" I persisted.

He just shook his head and said, "I'm sorry, Mrs. Madruga, but I've shown you what's available to the radical amputee."

After thanking the man, I grabbed my crutches and left that room, left that building as fast as I could. I had to get out of that alien world of artificial hands, arms, legs, noses, ears, and breasts; away from the smell of glue, the incessant hammering, and the sawdust.

I refused to accept this scene in which I had just played the leading role of the victim. It was all too bizarre, unreal; that world of exposed nuts and bolts, and wooden legs. I wanted to be a part of the real world; the normal world where everyone had two legs. If I had to wear an artificial limb, then it would be a real life-like leg.

"I'm not going to wear that thing!" I kept repeating as we made our way out to the parking lot. I was angry, disappointed, disillusioned. "I'm not going to wear anything that looks like that and nobody's going to force me!" I cried with tears of anger and frustration streaming down my face.

"I'm going to find a Barbie-doll leg. Someone, somewhere, will make me a beautiful and shapely Barbie-doll leg!"

Our next appointment *was* in one of the worst parts of town. We hurriedly parked the car and rushed into the building trying to avoid the derelicts loitering at the entrance.

The prosthetist who greeted us was a small, happy fellow of Italian descent. He cheerfully and proudly showed us around his spacious shop. The cabinets which lined the workshop were filled with mechanical arms and legs; some plastic, some with a foam covering, and some wooden. I felt as though I was in the workshop of Geppetto, the woodcutter, and that he and his men were building arms and legs for puppets like Pinocchio to dance and entertain the children.

"Geppetto" introduced us to one of his fellow "woodcutters," a man who was a below-the-knee amputee. The man wasted no time in demonstrating to us how he could walk, sit, bend, even dance. We were amazed at his maneuverability, his adroitness, his mastery of a limb that he had only worn for two years. When I asked him how he lost his leg, he smiled and with a twinkle in his eye, said, "I lost it in a poker game!"

At the front of the shop was a retail area which featured over-sized brassieres, uplifted shoes, canes, crutches, bed pans, and wheelchairs that appeared to be suspended in mid-air as they hung precariously from the ceiling. I realized that this vast assortment of implements for the disabled represented a strange new world that I, unwillingly, was now a part of.

After the grand tour, I explained that I needed to have a beautiful yet functional leg. I told him what I had already seen that morning. I warned him that if that was the only type of limb that he could offer me, then I might as well leave right then so as not to waste his time or mine. He listened intently as I described the big harnessed leg. He said that he could build a prosthesis without the harness, but the bucket was absolutely necessary because it was the only thing that the artificial limb could attach itself to. In anticipation of my visit he had asked a patient of his to come in and meet me. He said that she too was a hemipelvectomy and that he had built a leg for her which she had been using for two years. I would better understand the mechanics of a prosthesis if I could actually see someone wearing and walking with one.

Margie was a middle-aged woman who was a little overweight, but who managed to get around quite adequately on her prosthesis anyway. Laboriously she walked toward me. She was wearing an ankle-length, white accordion-pleated skirt. On her feet were what appeared to be little pink ballerina slippers. I was panic-stricken by her attire. Would I have to wear a skirt like that? Why was she wearing those slippers? I used to wear high heels. Would I have to wear such slippers?

As Margie proudly lifted up her skirt to show me her leg I was surprised that it was not made of wood. Instead it looked like a stocking that had been overstuffed with cotton. It was foam, I was told, with a cosmetic covering to make it appear more life-like. I liked the softness, but I didn't like the shape or the overstuffed effect. Before I had a chance to ask why the leg had that peculiar shape, Margie immodestly picked her dress up over her head and showed me how the bucket strapped around her hips. I noticed that the bucket was in sections and asked the prosthetist why.

He explained that this offered more maneuverability to the patient. He asked Margie to turn around and show us the back end of the bucket. I was surprised to see a deep concave area on the left side of the bucket. I knew, of course, that her buttock had been brought around somewhat because of her amputation, but why couldn't the bucket be filled on that one side, rounded out to simulate Margie's original buttock and match up with her right one? "Geppetto's" explanation was that cosmetic construction on the bucket had not yet been developed.

I badgered Margie with questions about clothing. I asked her what sizes she had to wear in order to hide the fact that she was wearing a bucket strapped around her hips. She said that she wore street-length or long, full dresses. Pants were obviously out of the question because of the indentation on the back side of the bucket.

I asked Margie if she would mind showing me how she walked. She threw her artificial leg unnaturally out to the side instead of in a more natural forward direction. I asked her why she didn't follow through with the leg. Why did she kick out to the side instead? She explained that in the beginning the prosthetist had taught her to kick to the front, but that it had proved too difficult because of the extreme weight of the prosthesis. She said she had no stump to aid her in kicking the leg out, which further hindered her from walking correctly. (I later found out that the only way a hemipelvectomy can force the swing of an artificial limb out is by using the strength of his back and lower back muscles.)

This palsied gait disturbed me the most. I persisted in questioning her on why she walked the way she did. I practically insisted that she make an effort to walk straighter. It was important to me that she walk normally, because I knew that I had to. Thankfully, Margie was a kind and patient woman; otherwise my demands would have seemed an affront instead of a projection of the fears I harbored.

The prosthetist said that it was possible for Margie to walk correctly if she would concentrate more on the technique of walking instead of just wanting to get somewhere quickly. Unabashedly, Margie said that she didn't care how she looked when she walked. It only mattered that she be able to walk and get around on her own. We differed on this point. I wanted to get around like Margie, but I wanted to do it in as normal a fashion as possible, and I wanted to look good at the same time.

Margie's leg was better. But it wasn't good enough. I didn't like the way in which the bucket was sectioned into parts, and I didn't like the way Margie was inclined to walk with it. There must be other places that would offer me something more.

"Why not go to Hollywood to buy a leg," LouAnn said after we left the shop. "Go to 'Tinseltown,' the city of dreams, where anything is possible. Go where the movie stars go. Follow the yellow brick road to the Land of Oz, where your every wish will be granted!"

"Maybe it's not such a bad idea," I said. "I have a cousin who lives in Los Angeles. I remember her saying that her boyfriend's mother is an orthopedic surgeon's nurse. Maybe she would know of a prosthetist in Hollywood. A wizard who could build me a proper Barbie-doll leg."

At the home of friends in San Francisco that evening, we laughed and joked about the artificial parts that we had seen on display. After a few glasses of wine, the disappointments of the day became comic scenes which we acted out with great hilarity. The grotesque machinery that had held us spellbound earlier now struck us as hysterically funny. Hilarious—until the moment I realized that the funny things we were laughing about were to become a vital part of me; an extension, a needed implement if I was ever to walk again.

The following day, after returning to Tracy, I went directly to Dr. Brakovec's office. I was mad. "Why," I demanded, "didn't you tell me that they don't make legs for people like me? Why," I pursued furiously, "didn't you have the guts to tell me that the only thing available for people like me is some big, old, ugly contraption that doesn't even look like a leg?"

"I'm sorry, Lenor," Dr. Brakovec meekly apologized. "But I honestly didn't know what might be available for a hemipelvectomy."

After I left Dr. Brakovec's office, I made several phone calls, and finally located Fred Karg, who had a shop in Hollywood. The nurse assured me that he was considered to be one of the best in the business.

I telephoned Mr. Karg and we talked at length about what I had seen and what I was seeking.

"I want to walk more than anything," I explained, "but I want an artificial leg that is not cumbersome or ugly. And I want a bucket that will be molded in the shape of my hips. Do you understand what I'm asking, Mr. Karg? Or am I asking the impossible?"

After I flew down to Hollywood and met with Fred Karg, I realized that he understood exactly what I wanted, and that my ideas were not unrealistic. We met not in his shop, but in the orthopedist's office. Fred Karg is a handsome man somewhere in his middle forties. A mass of disheveled hair outlines a kind and intelligent face. He speaks softly, but with deep conviction. From the moment I met him I knew God had answered my prayers. I would be normal again! I would look good again! I would walk again!

Fred recalls: "I thought your ideas on what your leg should look like were imaginative and unique. I personally had never built a leg such as you requested, but because of your enthusiasm and your determination, my interest developed. You had visions of toenails, toes, life-like texture, feel and shape, suddenly you presented a challenge to me. A challenge that I decided to meet. I became determined to meet your criteria; to build a shapely, functional, yet not cumbersome leg for you. Your primary interest in the beginning was that the leg look good. You took for granted that you would walk again, so that was of secondary importance."

Fred was correct in his assumption that I wanted a pretty leg first and foremost. It never entered my mind that I would have a problem learning to walk with an artificial leg. Fred said that because of my personality, my drive, and my determination in looking good again and wanting to walk again, he was totally convinced that I was going to do my part, and that was why he was willing to undertake the job.

Fred then measured and examined me. He was exceedingly pleased that the doctors were able to save the crest of my hip. I was not a true hemipelvectomy, he said. What I had left was called a "hemi-hemi" which means a half of a hemipelvectomy. He explained that a true hemipelvectomy has lost the entire half of the pelvic bone. Fortunately, because I was left with the crest of my hip, an artificial limb could attach itself to the pelvic bone structure.

Fred kept referring to my wound as a "stump." I told him that I hated the word and was going to find another to describe my amputation. Most amputees felt the same, he said; even prosthetists abhorred the word. When I finally found my new word—modilimb—Fred said that he would begin to use it immediately with his patients. He had been to a prosthetists' convention, where they had also been trying to find a word to replace "stump." That group came up with "residual limb."

After we had gone over everything I was completely

convinced that he was the "wizard" who could fulfill my dreams. I agreed to go to his shop the following day to have my hips molded in plaster of Paris so that he could get a master mold that would be the ultimate shape of my bucket.

LouAnn and I arrived at Fred's small shop around nine o'clock in the morning. To my utter shock and dismay the little shop was located on a boulevard that was lined with pornographic book stores and adult theatres; all advertising some sort of sordid entertainment. LouAnn and I rushed into the shop almost running head on into Fred Karg. I was immediately put into a small room. It was sectioned off from the working area by a curtain. I then disrobed so that Fred could begin the process of wrapping my hips with rags smeared with plaster-of-Paris.

As I stood on one leg for a good forty-five minutes, I welcomed the warmth of the gooey rags that were individually and painstakingly wrapped around my hips. The heat and support soothed my phantom pain. The rags dried in a short period of time, and after they were removed a perfect shell had been created of my hips. Fred said that he wouldn't need to see me now for another two weeks. It would take that amount of time for him to fabricate the rest of the prosthesis, so I returned to Tracy for a restless wait.

The two weeks finally ended—I was off. Jane Johnson, a former high-school classmate of mine, volunteered to fly down with me and spend the additional two weeks it would take to be fitted for a prosthesis. There was never any question or discussion about whether or not my husband would accompany me. By his silence, I knew that he acknowledged and understood my reasons for going on my own. Before my surgery I had always cherished my independence, and I was determined that the sudden loss of my limb would not imprison that free spirit. It was important that I prove to my husband that I could still be independent with or without a leg.

There was another reason why I didn't want Joseph to travel south with me. I had been told that the fitting, adjusting, and aligning involved in the making of a new prosthesis and the therapy involved in learning to walk would take patience, stamina, and courage. I didn't want Joseph to be subjected to any more of my frustrations. He had already paid his dues; in hospital waiting rooms, recovery rooms, and doctors' offices. I wanted to spare him any more grief—it was enough!

I had visions of returning home with a new leg; walking off the plane, unassisted, into the waiting and eager arms of my husband. I wanted to be me again, whole again, walking again. It was my only concern; my only future.

I was afraid the morning we left for the airport on that hot, sultry morning in August. I was suddenly gripped by the uncertainty of what awaited me at the end of our journey and I was on edge, like a cat.

Jane recalls: "When we arrived at Burbank Airport some sixty minutes later, we were suddenly faced with getting luggage, seeing to a taxi, getting to our hotel and unpacking. With the burden of your crutches, you didn't have enough arms or legs to take care of the traveling incidentals that most people take for granted. I told you to sit on a nearby bench, and that I would take care of everything. You didn't resist. You sat down, but the look of helplessness never completely left your eyes until the following morning when you met the prosthetist, Fred Karg."

When we reached the hotel, before we even had a chance to put our things away, I suggested that we go swimming. I explained to Jane that the cold water and a vigorous swim were two things that would offer immediate relief to my merciless nerve endings. We quickly changed into our bathing suits and cover-ups and proceeded to take the elevator up to the sixth floor where the pool was located.

It was only after we reached the pool and secured two lounge chairs that it suddenly occurred to me that in moments I would be giving my first public showing of me in a bathing suit, before the beautiful people of Los Angeles.

Heretofore, my long cover-up had hidden the fact that something about me was very different. I hesitated in disrobing because of my self-consciousness, and because I knew that I would shock everyone around the pool. While I was vacillating, Jane removed her cover-up, revealing a spectacular figure, unblemished and unchanged since our high-school days. Her brief bikini, to my dismay, only accentuated her long slim legs.

"Legs, legs, why are they so important?" my vanity cried out. "And why are Jane's legs so beautiful, so perfect?" Not wanting Jane to notice my sudden envy, I tried to make a joke of our predicament. "Well, you may have the best legs in town, Jane, but I've got the best boobs!" We both burst out laughing releasing the emotional pressure that had slowly developed since our arrival at the pool.

"Well, one person can't have everything, can one?" Jane retorted.

Given confidence by Jane's quick rationale, I whipped off my cover-up and dove into the pool ignoring the surprised, aghast expressions I knew were all around me. All of my inhibitions were drowned once I hit the cool, soothing pool water. I swam joyously, vigorously, lap after lap. Not understanding, but caring even less, why it was that when I swam I felt as if my other leg was with me. The only thing that mattered to me that moment was that

I was able to swim, that I was free from pain, and free from the ugly, gawking stares that followed me.

As I swam, I found myself wanting to change the pitying stares to looks of a more positive nature. I began to swim with all my heart, faster and faster, harder and harder. Curtains were being opened above me from the rooms that overlooked the pool. People were calling others to come and look at this unbelievable exhibition. I found myself suddenly enjoying the attention. I began to show off. With as much grace and form as I could manage, I attempted underwater ballet, flips, and dives from the side of the pool. I was Esther Williams. I was a woman with two legs performing for my adoring fans.

I became even more brave, when I decided to swim underwater to the other end of the pool, where I suddenly emerged in a spray of water directly in front of a group of startled men who had been eyeing me. With a big smile and a shake of my "tail," I said, "I'll bet you fellows thought I was a mermaid!"

"Oh, no, no, no," they all blurted out simultaneously. When they saw that I was amused by their attention and not offended, they proceeded to apologize for openly staring at me. They tried to explain that they couldn't help but look because they were astonished at how well I could swim.

One of the men asked if he could help me out of the pool. I thanked him but told him that I would need my crutches which were on the other side of the pool with my friend. He told me not to worry, that he would first assist me to a chair and then he would go get my crutches and my friend. I held on to his arm and hopped where he led me, among all his friends. I caught a glimpse of Jane shaking her head in amusement. After the man introduced me to his friends, he retrieved my crutches and Jane. I could sense that everyone was a little uncomfortable as I sat in the midst of them with only one leg. I immediately assumed the responsibility of putting everyone at ease. It was important that I make an effort to forget my condition, to not draw attention to it, so that the others would not feel the need to comment, to pity, or to condescend. I found that I am accepted as an equal only when I can assume this confident manner.

My mermaid anecdote has become a way of motivating other amputees, especially young females. Single girls, I've found, who are suddenly victims of an amputation, have a very difficult time adjusting. They all ask the same questions: "Who will look at me now? How will I ever find a husband?" They truly believe that no man will ever want them or even look at them again. They have fears that they will not be able to compete with other girls who have two legs and are unmarred by the ravages of a scalpel. "Why would a man choose half of a woman when he could have a whole woman?" is the most poignant question I am asked.

I don't have all the answers for these girls, or even for myself, but I do believe that the loss of a limb need not rob a person of her attractiveness or her dignity. I've tried hard to use my situation as a source of strength. A man recently said to me, "You're a beautiful woman, but beautiful in more ways than one." I think he meant that my acceptance of my circumstance had transformed into an inner beauty which was visible even to strangers.

We arrived at Fred's shop punctually at 8 A.M. the next day. He greeted us and asked us to wait in one of the small examining rooms while he went to get my leg.

"You mean you've actually got my leg ready?" I asked in disbelief.

He told me that only the skeleton was ready, and that he would be right back in a moment to show me. What seemed to me to be an eternity, but was only a few seconds, he returned. I was unprepared to see what he was carrying. It was a skeleton all right, but an aluminum skeleton of my future leg with steel pylons, springs, and wires attached to it. My heart sank at the sight of it. Where was the life-like leg he had promised me with shape and form? Where was my Barbie-doll leg?

Fred could see that I was stunned, and proceeded to calm me with assurances that after he had a chance to align the leg to my body and adjust it to my gait (almost like aligning bones to one's body, he explained), then he would cosmetically cover the skeleton with a foam-like covering that would be shaped exactly like my right leg. And then he would have a rubber-like covering put over it that would be painted and matched to my skin tone.

"But more important than the aesthetic beauty of your leg, Lenor," Fred said, "is getting to work on adjusting and aligning the leg so that you can walk first."

We did get to work. For the next three days I arrived early each morning at the shop and between adjustments visited the back working areas watching, in fascination, while Fred and his men worked on the intricate mechanisms that formed feet, ankles, knees, thighs, hands, and arms. These ingenious men were able to shape limbs into every conceivable shape and size. Fred did on-sight sculpturing like an artist who paints a picture from a model. From merely looking at a patient's leg, he could sculpt a foam blob into the exact dimensions of the patient's other leg.

Fred told me that many times a patient does not want a replica of their other leg. Many women want their artificial leg to be shaped slim and attractive. He said he has a difficult time sometimes convincing an overweight woman that it would be disproportionate to shape the leg slim if her remaining leg was large.

Every day I would sit on a high stool and ask a million questions of Fred and his men, while they diligently worked on my leg. In the beginning it was difficult to dissociate myself from the real world, to this doll-like, fantasy world of artificial parts. But its make-believe aura quickly became reality whenever I saw these toy-like implements suddenly enable a limbless man to walk again or an armless woman to be whole again.

One day I saw something standing in a corner of the room that reminded me of the grotesque apparatus that I had first seen in San Francisco. In horror, I asked Fred what kind of deformity warranted a thing like that. He said that it was for a thalidomide deformity. What I was looking at was the future leg of a thalidomide baby who had reached his seventeenth birthday.

The next morning Fred said that I was going to have my first lesson in walking. The moment the bucket was securely strapped around my hips I could feel my nerve endings relaxing in response to the support that the bucket offered. I sat down so that he could fit my shoe to the prosthesis, then I was asked to stand up. I couldn't get up. The strange thing that now encompassed my hips wouldn't let me move—let alone stand up.

Fred assisted me to my feet. The leg seemed to weigh a ton. The bucket seemed bulky and stiff like a strait jacket. To my bewilderment it not only covered my hips, but reached almost up to my bustline. I couldn't even bend. How, I thought, will I ever be able to pick anything up, sit, or stoop? I cast a quick anxious glance at Fred who quelled my apprehension by telling me that the excess plastic could be trimmed down to my waist, after he was confident that I could balance myself sufficiently, without the added extension. He asked me first to balance myself on both legs. After I balanced myself as best I could, Fred urged me to take my first step.

"I can't kick it out," I said after several exasperating tries.

"Use your back muscles, Lenor. Throw your leg out with the strength of those muscles. Just take it a step at a time, Lenor."

"One step at a time," I whispered; "one step at a time," I repeated, as I took my first step and then my next.

"Fortunately," Fred said, "your head was in the right place that day you took your first steps. A positive mental attitude is the most important thing for a patient to have the day he takes his first steps. The artificial leg has no motor. It's not electrically powered. It's only a tool that the patient must make work, make move, make walk. It can only give as much output as you give input."

I supported myself by holding on to the railing with one hand and my crutch with the other. He said I would probably use my crutches as an aid for the next two or three months. I didn't want to stop. I kept slowly taking step after step. Suddenly, without warning, the leg gave way and I fell to the ground. It was the most frightening sensation I've ever felt in my life. I felt like Alice in Wonderland, helplessly falling, falling, not understanding how or why I was falling.

Fred, unaffected by my fall, helped me back up. He said that my knee had collapsed, and that it was nothing to worry about.

"Nothing to worry about," I thought wildly. "What does he mean? I had faith in that leg, I believed it to be strong, steady, indestructible."

He continued to explain that when I stepped down, the knee had not locked. It was important to use my body weight to secure the lock and how that for now I must always look down, to make sure that it was locked. After a time it would not be necessary to look down, I would automatically sense the locking and unlocking of the knee.

I psyched myself into trusting this imposter. I began to put more and more weight on it. I experimented with the knee; locking it, unlocking it with each step. I was wondrously ecstatic because I was standing upright, straight on my "own two feet." My enthusiasm was dampened only by the gigantic mirror at the other end of the room which glaringly reflected the aluminum skeleton that was assuming the place of my missing leg. Fred kept telling me not to worry about what it looked like. He told me to just concentrate on walking. So I blocked my eyes, my mind, my heart, to the sight of that robot-looking thing that was strapped to me. I concentrated only on taking one step at a time.

After a few more days of therapy Fred said that he was satisfied that the prosthesis was adjusted properly to my gait and to my body. He was now ready to shape the foam that was to become the configuration of my left leg. After the leg was shaped and covered cosmetically, he said we would then venture out on the street to try to negotiate curbs, sidewalks, going in and out of doors, up and down stairs, and crossing streets.

For two days I sat perched high atop my stool in the workroom, while Fred painstakingly and patiently shaped an enormous blob of foam that looked like a circus fat lady's leg, into a shapely leg. He used a routing machine to sculpt the blob into a perfect size 6½ medium foot. He shaped each toe individually, an ankle, a knee with dimples, and a thigh (no dimples, please). As he scrupulously eyed my right leg, I tried to position it so that it would appear long and slim. Yes, like the other vain women, I, too, wanted a beautiful leg. I knew I hadn't fooled him when he matter-of-factly explained that it wouldn't make any difference if he made the left leg bigger than the right one. In months my one remaining leg would increase dramatically in size because it would have to bear the load of two legs.

When we were satisfied with the form and shape of the leg Fred slipped it on over the skeleton. To my relief, it no longer looked like the circus lady's leg, but an identical twin to my right leg.

His next step was to shape the buttock. He glued a large piece of foam to the left side of the bucket. He then shaped the left cheek to the exact dimensions of my right cheek.

After trimming the brace down to my waist, he was ready for the final touch—the cosmetic covering of the prosthesis. Because I insisted that the covering look like real flesh, Fred called in a Mr. Peyton Massey, who is well known in the film world for his knowledge of cosmetic coverings for prostheses. He had designed the arm for the "six million dollar man" for television; an artificial eye for Jimmy Stewart in *Fool's Parade*, and an array of distorted-looking eyes, ears, and noses for Marlon Brando in different films.

Mr. Massey used a life-like plastic for the skin which covered the entire leg. He sprayed it with a pigmented plastic to the exact skin tones of my right leg. My toenails were painted with my favorite pink polish.

I put the leg on, in front of Fred and Mr. Massey. As I viewed my reflection in the mirror the total effect was breathtaking. I was no longer wearing a robot's appendage; I was standing on my own two beautiful legs. I could tell from the delighted expressions that Fred and Mr. Massey were as pleased as I was with their unique creation.

Unhesitantly, I thanked God for this miracle, and in the same breath I thanked Fred and Mr. Massey.

"It's beautiful," I cried out. "It's exactly what I had

envisioned. It's my Barbie-doll leg." I looked at myself in the mirror from every angle. I could hardly make out any difference between my right cheek and my left. It was extraordinary; it was beyond belief!

I asked Fred if I could wear pantyhose over all of this. He said absolutely yes, and offered to put them on me. Jane graciously lent her own pair for me to try on.

Fred had a great deal of difficulty putting the sheer pantyhose on my legs. I heard him cursing under his breath, and finally he said that maybe I could figure out how to put them on by myself. I accepted the challenge and began tugging and pulling at the pantyhose. Whenever I was sitting down, the foam covering the leg would tighten and become inflexible. Fred had said in time the foam would lose its elasticity and stretch so that I could manipulate it more easily. Jane doubled over with laughter, saying that I looked like a contortionist performing a strange exhibition. It didn't matter because, after I finally managed to get the hose up over both legs and around the brace, after so many months of wearing one cut-off pair, I was at last wearing a full set of pantyhose like any normal woman.

Then I began to practice walking. The hardest thing for me to get used to, in the beginning, was the tremendous weight of the limb. Twelve pounds of steel, plastic, and foam strapped around my 95-pound frame seemed more than I could handle. And yet I had to do the impossible. I had to give it life and mobility. Not having a dangling modilimb made the task all the more difficult.

Fred kept encouraging me to use my back muscles and my pelvis to thrust the leg out. Surprisingly—wonderfully, my new limb eased my phantom pain. The contoured shape of the bucket offered support to my modilimb, thus alleviating the pain. And, because I was concentrating on walking, I no longer was focusing my attention on the phantom pain.

Incredibly, when I took a step, I could actually feel my nonexistent foot hit the ground. The jar of hitting the ground would jolt the artificial leg just enough to stimulate my nerve endings at the site that corresponded to my lost foot! Even when my foot was firmly planted on the floor, that little bit of pressure would alert my nerve endings to the foot's exact location without my having to look down.

On my last scheduled day at the clinic, Fred said we were ready to go for our little walk on the street.

"But I leave tomorrow. How will I learn to step off curbs, cross streets, and do all the other things you mentioned by tomorrow?" I asked incredulously.

He said that there were some things that even he couldn't teach me to do. Only constant practice would enable me to walk well with my prosthesis. Most of the other things like getting in and out of cars or dancing I must learn on my own. Only I could respond to how the prosthesis functioned. He could teach me basics, but nothing more. He assured me that my home was as good a practice area as Hollywood.

With only crutches in hand for assistance, we proceeded toward the door. My first obstacle: the door swung open automatically when I stepped on the mat and swung closed very quickly. Fred said all I had to do was coordinate my walking speed with the swinging of the door.

"But I can't walk that fast, Fred," I said in a panic.

"Oh yes you can; if you want to get out through that door you will quicken your pace."

Walking with as much speed as I dared, I made it out the door, heaving a sigh of relief. We started walking. Fred drew my attention to the uneven surfaces of the sidewalk below, warning me to watch out for those differences because the slight changes in the concrete could keep my knee from locking securely.

As we continued our little walk I smiled to myself at the unlikely location in which I was learning to take my first steps. I had imagined that my therapy would take place in either gleaming hospital corridors or sunny physical-therapy rooms, not on a deteriorating street somewhere in Hollywood. Barkers were calling from doors of dingy little neon-lit shops. Women of every age and every size were soliciting on street corners.

Stepping off curbs was the most difficult thing for me to learn. I feared leading off with my fake foot, as Fred instructed. I didn't have the confidence, as yet, in its ability to fully support me and not collapse from under me. Stepping off like that gave me the sensation of stepping off into limbo. It took courage to force myself off the curb each and every time. Crossing streets was easy enough. Getting to the other side before the green light changed was my only difficulty. After about 30 minutes of street therapy we returned to the shop and Fred said that he felt that I was ready to pack up my leg and go home.

"Pack up my leg!" I exclaimed. "But I want to wear it home like I had promised I would. I want Joseph to see me walking off the plane."

Fred wisely discouraged me from wearing my prosthesis home. He said I needed a little more practice before I attempted getting on and off planes.

Fred said it might be easier to come in the next morning on our way to the airport and pick up the leg instead of taking it back to the hotel. We agreed. Jane and I got in a taxi and headed back to our hotel.

"Let's go shopping, Jane, and find me the prettiest pantsuit in town," I said.

Since my surgery, I had never—not even in the privacy

of my bedroom—tried on a pair of pants. The mere thought of wearing slacks and not being able to fill the other pant leg was inconceivable. But now that I had another leg to fill that void, I was determined to buy a pair of tight-fitting slacks and model them the next day for Fred and his crew before leaving for home. At a boutique near our hotel I found a beautiful blue knit pantsuit and without even trying it on I purchased it. (How could I, anyway, when my other leg was back at the shop?)

The next morning at the shop, Jane and I went into the little examining room and she helped me with the leg, as it was still very difficult for me to fasten it on alone. I sat down and she then assisted me with the pants and then the blouse. After I had tucked the blouse into my pants, I noticed that my waist looked thick. It was caused by the way in which the brace curved outward from my waist. Fred had already explained to me that the brace was designed in this way so it would not cut into my waist. And because the plastic surrounding my waist was sensitive to body heat, it caused the brace to roll over away from my waist. I was thankful that the brace did give. The protrusion was annoying, but at least it was hidden by the jacket.

There I stood, in a pair of size 10 pants. I couldn't believe that I actually looked attractive and shapely in my new pantsuit. I "sauntered" out of the examining room. I was exhilarated—I looked fashionable again! Fred and his men stopped everything and looked up at me. First one, and then the others began to applaud. After the fashion show, Fred said he would wrap the leg up securely in a bag so that we would be able to carry it aboard the plane and so it would not end up damaged in the baggage chutes.

The moment finally came for me to say thank you and

goodbye to Fred and his men. How could I express thanks to a man who had given me mobility, freedom, and pride? It was difficult. I felt more than just respect for this man. I felt deep affection for and devotion to him because he was able to achieve the difficult task of making me whole again—making me walk again.

We boarded the plane just a few minutes before take-off. The stewardess could find no place to put the long bulky bag.

"How about standing it up front in the cockpit?" I suggested.

"Why not?" she said and carried it up the aisle.

On the way out at the end of the flight we went up front to collect the bag. We greeted the pilots and I asked the captain if he would be kind enough to help me get the bag off the plane.

"Certainly," he said. "What is it, a sculpture?"

"No, it's my other leg," I grinned. He turned and swung my leg over his shoulder. As he walked down the portable stairway he looked back at the co-pilots and stewardesses who were all watching, and winked. "Well if you can't have the whole woman, you might as well take a part of her!"

Family portrait: my mother, myself, my brother Ernie, sister Diane

At two years old, in Chino, California

My husband-to-be, Joseph, and I at a high-school dance, 1955

Here I am on the porch of our newly restored home

On vacation in Mexico, before
I discovered the lump

At the Mayo Clinic, Easter
Sunday, 1974

Family portrait, Christmas, 1974: I insisted Joseph sit. I wanted my relatives and family to see me standing on my new leg.

In the kitchen with daughters Christianna, 10, and Daniella, 7

On horseback at the ranch

Waterskiing, San Joaquin Delta, 1978

Showing off my matching pair of legs, 1978

Using my new leg: dancing with my husband Joseph

Portrait with Joseph

Out on a Limb

I will tell no one
How long I stopped to weep
Soon I will reach the top

The children must have seen us coming up the driveway from the window, for they were already out the door before the car had even stopped, followed by Annabelle and Joseph.

"Where's your other leg, Mom? Where's your new leg?" they cried as they hugged and tugged at my leg.

"In the back seat of the car," I said with a wink. "In the brown paper bag."

Annabelle, emotionally, held me and kissed me. Joseph in his usual undemonstrative manner brushed my lips quickly with a kiss, then busied himself by carrying the luggage into the house.

I could find no proper way to thank Jane for the two weeks she spent with me in a strange city, offering help at every turn, encouraging me to walk, and tirelessly massaging me to ease my pain. She had given of herself unselfishly—her only reward was to witness my first steps, and that, she said, was enough.

I then unveiled the "Karg masterpiece" for my expectant family. Christianna said excitedly, "Mommy, it's not a silver leg, or a polka-dotted leg like I dreamed it would be. It's a real leg, Mom, just like your other one. I love it!"

Daniella liked the toes and the pretty pink nail polish. The children accepted it immediately as Mom's other leg. They especially loved how it could stand in the corner of the room, as if of its own volition. Annabelle found looking at the life-like limb very upsetting. And she wondered how I would ever be able to walk with it. It looked too bulky for my small frame.

Joseph admired it from a mechanical point of view, thoroughly impressed by the way the knee was able to bend, the shape and design of the bucket, and the cosmetic covering. He marveled at Mr. Massey's faithful reproduction of my tanned right leg.

"Put it on, put it on," were the cries of my children. "Show us how it walks."

"Tomorrow, girls. Mommy is a little tired now, but tomorrow I will show you how it walks. I promise."

I did not keep my promise to my daughters. Tomorrow came and went, and the next day, and the next. I consciously ignored the prosthesis that stood beckoning, challenging me from its corner of the living room.

It seemed that I had lost my spirit, my energy, my will—something was missing. Maybe it was because I didn't have Fred standing over me, instructing me, encouraging me to put the brace on, to get used to it, to walk with it. "I had already accomplished that anyway," I thought to myself. "What more did I have to prove?"

I needed a little time to regain my strength from the trip—that was one of my excuses. It was easier and faster to get around on my crutches, was another excuse. The weight of the thing was discouraging, and it was the hottest time of the year, was my final excuse. It would be better to wait until the weather cooled off before I strapped on the hot, suffocating prosthesis.

Much later, I was to find out that making up excuses or reasons not to wear their prosthesis is a common pattern amputees fall into. A large percentage of amputees who come home with a new prosthesis put it into a closet and forget about it. Many of the amputees one sees crutching around or being wheeled around have a prosthesis hidden away in some dark corner. This is especially true of radical amputees, because their prostheses are so weighty and cumbersome. If an amputee does not put his prosthesis on soon after it's built and does not wear it from morning until night, he will soon abandon it forever.

Fred explained to me once the crippling alternatives I would have faced if I had not been fitted for a prosthesis soon after my amputation and worn it faithfully. Severe scoliosis—curvature of the spine—most likely would have developed; arthritis could have set in; discs may have slipped, necessitating a spinal fusion. I would have become lopsided.

Some people can't afford to buy a prosthesis, Fred noted, and there are some—a very small percentage however—who have such a bad condition that you just can't put a leg on them. But that percentage is tiny. "I have only known maybe one or two amputees in my entire career who could not be fitted with a prosthesis."

Why then do some amputees choose not to wear their limbs, in light of the devastating alternatives? Some enjoy the pity that is suddenly bestowed upon them. But most, like me, want to avoid dealing with that ambivalence— the desire to walk again versus the reluctance to undertake yet another demanding physical task, yet another long, arduous adjustment in the way I moved around.

After the leg had stood unused in the corner for three days, Joseph suggested that I put it on. From the tone of his voice I knew that it was more of a command than a suggestion.

I reluctantly agreed. Joseph carried it up the stairs and into our bedroom. I asked him to leave while I put it on. I wasn't quite ready for him to witness the struggle I knew I would have putting the leg on for the first time by myself. Joseph leaned the leg up against the bed and left. I sat on the bed for a while just looking at it. "It is beautiful," I thought to myself, "so life-like. If only it wasn't so difficult to manipulate and if only it wasn't so heavy."

Fred did say that one day it would become an extension of my body—like a real working part. But he said I would have to wear it every day so that I could adapt myself to it. Even if I just strapped it on and sat in it, it would help me to become accustomed to its feel, its weight.

I stood up, grabbed the leg and stood it up beside me. I then eased my hips into the bucket. After my hips were comfortably housed, I strapped it up. The next step was pantyhose. Slipping them on the left leg was fairly easy, but to put them on the right leg posed a problem. I had to stretch and bend against the stiffness of the bucket to reach that right foot. I finally made it and pulled them up to my waist. Then shoes: first the shoe on the left foot; then the shoe on my right. That was easy enough.

I had to sit down again to put the pants on. Bad leg first, good leg second. I stood up to pull the pants up over the brace and zipped them up. I picked a blouse that would cover the ridge at the waist of the brace and my chore of dressing was accomplished. Just like a child, I had to learn all over again how to dress myself. The energy it took to get dressed and put the leg on left me perspiring and breathing heavily. It was hard work. It would take many months before I would become adept at performing this normally easy task of putting myself together.

I called down to Joseph to come upstairs and help me down. He hadn't even reached the top of the landing when I could see the pleased expression on his face— seeing me dressed in pants and standing on my own two feet! To see his face light up like that was worth all the effort and frustration of getting the darn thing on.

Joseph handed me my crutches and told me to go downstairs where I could practice walking better. He said he would take the lead down the stairs just in case I started to fall.

After the loss of my leg, etiquette became secondary

in importance to necessity. Going downstairs, for instance, Joseph takes the lead just in case I should fall; he follows me going upstairs for the same reason. He leads the way through doors to make sure no obstacles are in the way. On the street, Joseph always walks on my left because it's easier for me to hold onto his arm with my left arm and use my right hand to work the cane.

Before taking my first step down the staircase, I tried to remember everything Fred had taught me about coming off a curb. With both crutches tucked under my left arm, one resting on the step below, and my right hand holding onto the railing, I stepped down with my left foot, secured the knee and followed with my right. That long flight of stairs was far more dangerous and difficult than stepping off a curb. However, taking it one step at a time with my dear husband guiding me, I made it down. Wow! Another feat accomplished.

I started walking around the house with the aid of my crutches, experimenting on different surfaces, locking and unlocking the knee. I walked on the living room carpet, the hardwood floors, and the kitchen linoleum; watching out for throw rugs, children's toys—anything that could obstruct my path. I stepped outside onto the brick front porch, and with the scent of fresh-cut alfalfa in the air, the lovely view of the surrounding mountains, and the sensation of both feet planted firmly on the ground, I realized I had come home. I had made it. Now, my next step was to get on to living a normal, active life.

I called Jack Royal, a physical therapist at our local hospital, and asked if he would give me some tips on walking. I wanted to get rid of the crutches as soon as possible; after all, I had a leg now—why did I need crutches? Jack said he had no experience in assisting an amputee to walk, but he agreed to do what he could.

The next morning I struggled to get dressed once again, but it was just a little bit easier than it had been the day before. And as the days passed it became less and less of an effort. My mother-in-law offered to take me to the hospital for my meeting with Mr. Royal. I thanked her but said I had to learn to drive the car with my prosthesis on, and that today was as good a day as any. She understood.

When I walked out to the car that morning, I automatically opened the driver's side and tried to slide over in my usual manner. It didn't work. The foam covering wouldn't give enough for the leg to get under the steering wheel. I picked up my crutches, which I had put in the back seat, and walked over to the passenger's side. The gravel driveway made my walk even more difficult. My foot could not hit the ground in a flat enough position for the knee action to lock. Walking very slowly and double-checking the knee, I made it to the other side of the car without any mishap. I opened the door and slid in backward keeping the leg in a straight position on the seat. When I reached the driver's side I was then able to bend the leg up sufficiently to put it under the steering wheel and situate it on the left side of the brake pedal.

I started the car and drove away. What a wonderful feeling it was to be driving my car again with two legs and two feet. It didn't take long for me to notice that the fake foot had to be secured on the left side of the floor board away from the brake pedal. The slightest turn of my body, like looking over my shoulder for another car, would move the foot under the brake pedal.

I almost had an accident some weeks later. I was coming to a stop sign and when I stepped on the brake pedal to stop, I got no reaction. I was almost into the busy intersection before I looked down and realized that my left foot was under the brake pedal. Naturally my frantic braking did nothing to alarm the poor little dummy foot all dressed up to look real. I braked to a screeching halt just in time to keep from being hit by a car.

The incident left me shaking and thinking, "I'll have to watch that foot." Another disturbing thought that entered my mind was: What if I was in an accident and the car caught on fire—how in the world could I jump out fast enough or even move fast enough away from the car? To this very day I have a dread fear of being caught in a car after an accident and not being able to get out in time.

I arrived at the hospital and drove, as always, as close as I could possibly get to the physical therapy entrance, to save steps and energy. Handicapped parking spaces are always a welcome sight to the disabled.

I got out of the car and made my way slowly to the entrance of the hospital. The door was heavy and difficult to pull open. My crutches hindered my efforts. Jack met me at the entrance. "I've simply got to get rid of these crutches," was the first thing I said to him.

Jack laughed and said, "Take it easy, maybe we can try you out on Canadian canes."

Jack tells me today that when I first called him he was excited and eager to work with a radically disabled person. He said he suggested getting off the crutches and onto canes not only because of my obvious frustration with the things, but also because of the severity of my condition. He felt that if I continued to use crutches I would become totally dependent on them, and the extreme pressure under my arms, which was exerted by my body weight, could cause irrevocable damage.

Before we even tried the Canadian canes—the kind with supporting bands that fit around the forearms—Jack gave me a preliminary examination. He checked for hip flexor tightness. Hip muscles, he explained, tend to shorten after an amputation. And if they have become

165

shortened, a program of passive-active-assistive hip flexor stretching exercises is necessary to increase the range of motion.

During the examination he found a great deal of tenderness around the hip, and some normal swelling. He checked the strength of my hip muscles and abdominal areas; both were very weak. If I didn't learn to walk and do it regularly, my muscles would soon lose their tone and my left side would sag.

While Jack adjusted the canes to my height, he explained that Canadian canes would be better for me than crutches, because they give forearm support which is less damaging than the underarm support. With Jack at my side, I proceeded to practice walking with my new canes.

As I cautiously walked down the halls, I remembered that not five months ago I had been in one of these very rooms awaiting a life or death verdict. Now, I was able to walk past my old hospital room, leaving behind the horrors and uncertainties of those terrible days and look, instead, to the future, to needing only one cane, and then one day—no cane!

At the end of the session, I shocked Jack by stepping out the door and into my car on the Canadian canes.

"I won't need my crutches anymore, Jack. Thank you!" I yelled out as I drove off.

After practicing for one week with the Canadian canes, I went to a standard cane. With one cane, now in hand, Jack said that I was ready to increase my functional abilities like side-stepping, stair climbing, getting in and out of a car in the proper fashion. In other words, he said, I was ready to develop proprioception. Proprioception means the knowledge of the position of the body and limbs without the use of vision. Normal people have this ability—due to special sensory nerves in the muscles. With the loss of a limb, normal proprioception is lost, also. After wearing the prosthesis for a while the neurological re-education begins. However, because the nerve endings in my modilimb were so sensitive, I still had, in a way, the neurological feedback of two legs. Perhaps this constant sensation was really a blessing instead of a wicked curse.

In the beginning it was difficult for me to get used to the feeling of only one walking cane, after the steady, sure support of crutches, and then later the forearm support of the Canadian canes. Suddenly I had to rely even more on my prosthesis—trusting it to perform as it should. Coming off curbs and going down stairs was even more frightening with only the support of a single cane. I had to believe in the efficiency of Karg's creation.

It was so unlike the Lenor of a few months before, always in a hurry, literally skipping down sidewalks, jumping off curbs. But because I was able to get to town on my own, walk down the city streets on my own, it didn't matter that I cut an unlikely figure of my old self. It only mattered that I could still do it.

I don't skip down streets today, but I do walk, and in a nearly normal fashion, consciously kicking the leg forward with every step—not to the side, which would be much easier. I still exert maybe double the energy of a normal person when walking, but my appreciation for the mere act of walking has doubled, too.

Because amputees must exert two to three times the energy of a normal person, they often become extremely fatigued, which leads to depression. I was exhausted after each day of practice with the canes—and I still get very tired after a day of walking—but instead of letting walking become an obstacle, I regarded it as a challenge. Jack felt that I was able to move from crutches to canes so quickly because, aside from the facts that I was young and in good health, I had a situation that I was in a hurry to return to: my husband, my children, and my work. This gave me the added incentive to walk or do whatever was necessary to return to a normal life. An amputee in other circumstances might not be so motivated. A man who is the breadwinner of a household but who doesn't like his job, for example, may have more difficulty learning to walk because it means returning to this unsatisfying job and resuming the support of his family. His drive to go back to what he used to do is sabotaged by the relief from the burdens his disability affords.

Suddenly summer was gone and the crispness of fall was in the air. Month after month I continued to make progress. It wasn't too long before I was able to walk without the use of my cane while doing household chores.

However, it has been important, then and today, for me to use a cane while out walking. It not only gives me added support and allows me to lean on it (in an effort to take some of the body weight off my modilimb, which becomes very aggravated when it must carry all the load), but it also offers a warning to others to beware. It alerts them to be careful when around me—not to push me or jostle me.

I searched everywhere for an attractive cane. Orthopedic shops were the only places that I could even find a cane. Finally, at the House of Canes in Westwood, I found a cane that is not only pretty, but much more stable as well. Instead of the standard curved handle, the new cane has a T-shaped handle which fits comfortably in the palm of my hand and allows me to grasp it firmly and stabilize myself.

The House of Canes had canes to suit every whim and fancy. The variety was extraordinary and the prices ranged from inexpensive to very expensive. I purchased a cane that looked like a riding crop and another one that was made of Lucite. Some canes had flasks in the handles; others had knives concealed in them; others had handles of solid gold, brass, or silver. One cane handle was shaped in the form of a hunting hound.

I was able to use my new canes not only for support but also as adornments. My canes with their intriguing handles and long sleek design appeared to be an accessory rather than a tool—an impression I like to give.

As the days passed and frost settled on the fields surrounding our house, the routine daily functions that I had to do became easier and easier. Wearing my prosthesis and going up and down the stairs became less of an effort. Doing the household chores only took half a day instead of the entire day. Cooking was so much quicker and less tiring on two legs rather than on one. At last, I was able to carry things to and from the table without having to dangle dishes and cups from hands which were already occupied with crutches. One of the most important reasons for me to wear my prosthesis was that it offered much-needed relief to my good leg. Whenever I got tired, I simply transferred all my weight to my fake leg.

The holidays were fast approaching. This would be the second year our family would be celebrating the holidays in our big, old comfortable house. I was determined that Christmas of 1974 was to be *no* different than the Christmas of 1973.

My friends couldn't understand why it was so important for me to do all the things that I was accustomed to doing. How could they understand the desperate need I had for everything to be like it was before I lost my leg? I wanted to cook, entertain, and join in on all the holiday festivities as I did before.

I began by decorating the house the first week in December. The children and I swagged holly up and down the staircases; ironed and fastened large red bows on it, intertwined little yellow lights over the old fireplace mantle, and placed poinsettias all over the living room in little red baskets. It was difficult and very tiring to stand for the many hours it took to decorate the entire house, but I did it. I wanted the house to have the same holiday cheer that it had had the year before.

After the house was decorated, I began my customary Christmas cooking, baking goodies for the children and gifts for my friends and neighbors. I sat on a stool whenever I was rolling out dough or doing anything that required standing in one place for long periods of time.

I also continued to produce fashion shows, which were expected to be much grander, more spectacular during the holiday season.

It was during the holidays, at a friend's party, that Joseph casually asked me to dance. The nagging fear of possibly not being able to dance with my prosthesis caught in my throat, as I rose to my feet and Joseph led me to where everyone was dancing. Our friends tried to be nonchalant and not stare as Joseph drew me into his arms and we started to dance. He held me tight, and I somehow managed to follow his every step. I was supported mostly by my good leg. However, whenever I felt secure enough in Joseph's embrace I would transfer the weight of my good leg to my bad leg.

We were dancing! Not with the grace, ease, or control as before; but with the same rhythm—the same euphoria I always felt while in my husband's arms. It was unbelievable to me that I was again dancing in a normal fashion; following my husband's every move and loving every minute of it.

After that first "lesson" with my husband, I became more and more adept at dancing. Rock, jitterbug, Latin, I tried them all. Our men friends began to lose their fears of what to do with me once they got me. They realized that if I could dance with Joseph, why not one of them? Each time I danced with a friend, his confidence would grow in my capabilities and in his ability to hold me up, lead me. When my good friend, Joe Salles, and I dance, people actually stop to gawk, as we effect quick turns, lean-backs, twirls.

When I dance with someone for the first time, it seems to me that they are very stiff and awkward, as if they had the wooden leg, not me. When dancing a slow dance, it's vital that my partner bring me very close, hold me firmly to his chest, and then just take the lead and let me worry about the following. Once they realize that I can follow and that I am not fragile, then we're able to enjoy dancing together.

Two years later, when Fred Karg came up to one of our annual Christmas parties, I asked him to dance with me. The more we danced the more Fred exclaimed, "I don't believe it! I don't believe it! If I hadn't built it myself I wouldn't believe it!"

It isn't often, I would imagine, that a prosthetist has the opportunity to dance with one of his inventions! Fred was overwhelmed with my dancing abilities and I was elated to be able to give life to the 12-pound contraption that adamantly clung to my hips—to make it perform, to do its best for its creator.

Yes, I can dance by exerting twice the energy of a normal person and by overstressing my one knee because of its solitary role as a pivotal point for my entire body. With the added burden of the dead weight of its mechanical partner, my right foot swells and a tingling sensation never leaves my foot for two or three days after I've danced all night. Oh, but to dance is worth the strain, the pain, anything! And I'm finding that the more I dance the more the painful after-effects are diminishing.

There is a loss, however, that can't be made up. I hate to admit it, but when my husband is dancing with another woman who is a good dancer, I am envious. Envious of her graceful movements, and her ease at following my husband's every step. His movements, too, seem less concentrated, less inhibited when he dances with her. Is it because he has no fear of his partner's knee collapsing out from under her? Is it because he has no 12-pound "dummy" to push around, to try to get some kind of response from? I cannot deny the irrepressible feelings that foment during those moments that my husband effortlessly glides another woman across a dance floor. Yes, there must be some things my husband misses, too.

Our Christmas party that year I thought to be even more exciting than it had been the year before. The thrill I felt at just being able to stand on two feet and greet our guests; to have prepared the buffet dinner entirely on my own; to watch my little daughters and their cousins all dressed up in their holiday best playing little hostesses; to see the happiness on my husband's face at having his family together; and being able to entertain our relatives and friends as we had always done in the past!

On Christmas eve, after putting the children to bed and reading *Twas the Night before Christmas* to them, I lingered for a while on the edge of their bed.

I was always glad that my children were of walking age when I came home from the hospital. How difficult it would have been had they been infants in diapers. However, I did miss carrying them around with me on my hip or in my arms, especially little Daniella, because she missed it so.

"Pick me up Mommy. Carry me," were the cries of Daniella, who was still a baby in so many ways. I would sit and hold her and try to compensate for not being able to carry this small child who wasn't old enough to understand why her mother could not carry her in her arms any more.

Why is it that, so often, we forget how important the little things in life are—like a simple motherly act of picking up a child? I never realized how much pleasure I derived from that one little gesture until I could no longer do it. Picking up the children from school each day used to be such a bothersome chore. Today, I thank God every time I'm able to drive to town on my own, sit, and wait if necessary, for my little girls to run from their classrooms to meet me. The joy of seeing them all rumpled and hot from the activities of the day, their book bags flying every which way, is indescribable.

After Christmas, Joseph and I rented a house on the beach for a week's vacation with a group of our friends.

When we arrived at the house, I had a sudden urge to feel the sand under my feet. I couldn't concentrate on unpacking. The ocean was roaring, pounding—calling me. As I continued to put things away, a consuming sadness came over me. A sadness closely resembling self-pity. "How will I be able to walk out there on the beach?" I asked myself. "It isn't fair. After all, I'm the only one besides Joseph, out of the whole group, who enjoys running on the beach and swimming in the ocean."

This kind of thinking, if nurtured, can destroy a person. I never spoke these thoughts aloud—not to my husband, not to anyone. I was too ashamed. How could I let anyone know that I was jealous that they had two legs? As I began to sink lower and lower into the depths of ugly self-pity, torturing myself with unanswerable questions, Joseph abruptly said, "Let's forget about the unpacking and go for a walk on the beach."

"Go for a walk on the beach!" I sarcastically repeated. "How can I go for a walk on the beach with this contraption hanging onto me? Besides, it will sink into the sand and I'll fall!"

"Possibly," Joseph said matter-of-factly. "And if you fall you will just have to get up and try again."

Hand in hand, Joseph and I walked down the overgrown path that led to the beach. Just getting down the path was difficult enough. My "funny" foot kept getting itself caught under the beach grass. Whenever it would get tangled, Joseph would nonchalantly "kick" it out of the bush.

Once on the sand, my foot was free of the grasping clutches of the grass, but sank in the sand the way a person's foot sinks in soft snow. The only way I could free the foot was by leaning way over on my right leg while bearing down on my cane.

When I finally got the rhythm of walking on the sand the going got easier if not any faster. I was walking on the beach, able to do something that only minutes ago I thought impossible.

Today, I'm able to walk alone on the beach. Even so, I still can't help but miss the tingling sensation of sand between my toes (because I must always wear shoes whenever I wear my prosthesis), or the glorious physical exertion of a good run on the beach.

It certainly wasn't warm enough to swim that day, but the sun was out and I wanted to see if I could still swim in the ocean. It could have been freezing and I think I still would have tried to dive into that inviting sea. Joseph thought I was crazy, but helped me back to the house so that I could change and get my crutches.

Crutching on the beach was much faster and easier than walking with my prosthesis, and I could feel the sand between my toes. Getting far enough out on crutches to be able to swim was my next dilemma. I crutched out as far as I could, threw my crutches back to shore, and dove into the surf. It was cold—ice cold, but it didn't matter because I was actually swimming in the ocean, riding the waves.

There were two important things I learned that day about swimming in the ocean. One was not to ride a wave too far into shore where the water is shallow. If I did get caught in shallow water I would become stranded in much the same way that a whale becomes beached when he ventures too far into shore. Like the whale, if I got caught in shallow water I could not swim back out to sea.

The other was to make sure when I wanted to return to shore that I wait for a wave to come along that is big enough to carry me all the way in, because there certainly was no way I was going to walk out.

After a time, Joseph motioned for me to come back to shore. I body surfed in on a wave that took me close to shore where Joseph waited with my crutches.

Two little boys who were playing in the sand looked up and innocently asked "What happened to your leg?"

"Sharks," I said.

In the house, I could not sit idly by while the other women did all the work. Each day two women would plan the menu (if we were going to stay home and eat), shop, cook, and clean up. The next day the other two women would try to surpass the previous day's menu. I was able to do my share, something that I knew I had to do. However, every once in a while whenever they would ask me to do something, I loved nothing better than facetiously saying, "Ask LouAnn, I'm handicapped." It never worked. They never, not then and not today, let me think of myself as "handicapped!"

Since my surgery I had not been around a normal, everyday working household besides my own. At the beach, I realized that I had forgotten how easy it was for my girlfriends to jump up and get a cup of coffee for their husbands. I noticed how easy it was for them to make beds, sweep floors, or just simply get around. I noticed, too, how easy it was for them to take naps in the afternoon, without having to remove a 12-pound brace. And when they awoke from their comfortable naps how they would saunter into the kitchen for a glass of wine or a cup of coffee, without having to worry about putting a leg back on just to walk into the kitchen. I bet they never in their entire lives appreciated just being able to walk from room to room until they lived with me for a week.

Another disconcerting thing for me was the fact that no one but I was in discomfort. I would ask God why I had to not only be without a leg but suffer pain as well. It's not that I wanted my friends to share my pain. I wanted them to appreciate how lucky they were to be free of consistent, nagging pain.

My New Year's resolutions for 1975 were to block these envious thoughts that I might have of others just because things are easier for them; to try to block from my mind the persistent phantom pain; to concentrate more on walking and the joy of being able to look forward to another year.

One day when we were shopping in town, Tony came running up to me. "I just saw a girl getting out of a taxi who looked like she had the same kind of operation as you," he said excitedly.

"How do you know that?" I asked.

"She isn't wearing a prosthesis, and she *is* wearing a crocheted miniskirt."

We caught up with her as she was coming out of a jewelry store with a group of her friends. I stopped her and asked if I could speak to her a moment.

My habit of stopping other amputees on the street has

continued to this day. I am always curious why some don't wear a prosthesis, why some prefer crutches, why some walk one way and others another way. There are still many questions that only another amputee can help me understand. Some people put up with my inquisitiveness. Others do not take kindly to my importunities.

This woman I stopped on the street in the beach town was beautiful. She seemed to be of Latin descent and was tall and slim. Her leg had been amputated above the knee, and her miniskirt exposed her modilimb. She couldn't believe that I was an amputee or that I was wearing a prosthesis. She kept asking me how I was able to wear a prosthesis with so high an amputation. She had lost her leg twenty years ago to bone cancer and had tried a variety of prostheses over the years, but with no success. They always collapsed on her, she explained; they were either too heavy, too clumsy, or too ugly.

She kept touching my life-like leg, scrutinizing it in fascination, in disbelief. I told her that if I could be fitted with a prosthesis, as radical as my surgery was, certainly she could, too. But she replied that because she had been disappointed so many times through the years with unsatisfactory prostheses, she had given up hope of ever being fitted. Nonetheless, her friends kept saying to her how wonderful it would be if she could walk without her crutches and urged her to get the name of my prosthetist. Just like a trained puppy, I did a few of my tricks for her, flexing my knee, walking, even throwing in a few dance steps.

I never heard from the woman again, and often wonder if she tried again to be fitted for a prosthesis. Probably not. Someone who has adjusted to living on crutches for twenty years usually would rather not go through the hassle of finding a workable, attractive leg. It's true that some amputees feel more agile without the weight of a prosthesis strapped to them, and some don't mind how they look with only one leg. But I always feel it's a pity that they won't know the freedom of not having hands full of crutches, the gratification of being able to walk into a room and not be stared at because you're on one leg, the confidence that comes from being able to wear clothes you like without having to pin or roll up a pant leg.

As the late winter and early spring months passed, I continued to learn how to do all the things that used to come so naturally to me and yet now presented great challenges. One afternoon, Joseph came home and asked if I would like to go for a ride with him out to one of the ranches where he had to make an irrigation change. We drove out to the ranch in Banta. Joseph stopped the pickup, got out, grabbed his shovel from the back of the truck, and as he started off, looked over his shoulder and said, "I'll be back in a minute, Honey. You can listen to the radio while I'm gone."

Ordinarily I would have jumped out and tagged along with him. But now because he felt it would be impossible for me to keep up with him, much less make it over ditch banks and trudge through the mud, he thoughtfully discouraged me by telling me to wait.

I was alone in the truck. The sun was setting while I watched Joseph walk away from me in his high hip boots with the shovel resting on his shoulder. As he lumbered down the ditch bank and his figure became smaller, I longed to be with him. I could feel my face becoming wet with the stirrings of self-pity slowly spilling from my eyes. I furiously wiped the tears from my face, threw open the heavy pickup door, and eased myself onto the ground below.

"I'm going to get up that steep ditch bank," I said under my breath, "and walk to my husband."

I started up the high embankment. As I bore down on my cane, I leaned to the right and with my good leg I was able to drag the "dummy" behind. I was almost in a crawling position as I arduously made my way up the dirt bank. At the top, I heaved a sigh of relief and looked toward my husband for some kind of acknowledgment. Joseph did not look up as he continued changing pipes. Even so, I sensed he was very much aware of my struggle and my need to reach him.

I started walking toward him carefully watching every step I took to make sure my knee locked, trying to avoid any obstacles which might keep me from reaching my husband. I finally made it. And when I got to him, he looked up and all he said was, "Hi, what took you so long?"

This inherent ability of Joseph's to hold back when he sees me struggling, sees me trying to accomplish something on my own has probably been the greatest stimulus to my rehabilitation. Sometimes I yearn for him to give in to my pain, my struggles, my disability. But he refuses. Never once has he allowed me to shirk my responsibilities or back off from challenges.

Sometime near my thirty-third birthday I called Fred up and told him that it was about time for me to start riding my horse again. I hadn't ridden in over a year, and even though I had no intention of getting back into barrel racing competition, I did want to ride once again.

My prosthesis afforded me the ability to walk but not the ability to cover great distances. In the evenings, often, I remember sitting on the front porch watching the brilliant sunset over the mountains and wishing that I could just get up and take off for a long walk down the lane and across the fields. I could physically take a long walk, of course, but it would be very strenuous. But on the back of a horse, I thought to myself, I could cover a lot of ground. I could even vicariously experience the sensation of running again.

I flew down to Los Angeles with a new traveling companion, my little daughter Christianna. Joseph was busy with spring planting. I didn't want him to come anyway; this was another thing I had to do on my own.

By the time I arrived at Fred's clinic he had already made a plaster-of-Paris cast of my original bucket. The skeleton of the new leg was already put together as well.

Fred wasn't sure that I would be able to ride a horse again. He said that if I did get on a horse, I would probably be one of the first hemipelvectomies to ever do so. Many amputees ride horses, he said, but they have a dangling modilimb, which affords them the support that a hemipelvectomy does not have. He explained that many prefer to ride without wearing a prosthesis because of the dangers of being hung up in the saddle, if thrown. But if an amputee has something left—even a few inches— he can ride without a prosthesis.

That first day in Los Angeles, we drove out to a riding stable somewhere in the Hollywood hills. Fred tried to assist me onto the back of a horse. It didn't work. The leg I wore would not extend out far enough to let me straddle the saddle. Fred said that he already knew that I wouldn't be able to sit in the saddle with my original leg. He just wanted to get some kind of idea of how much to extend and align my new leg. He measured the width of the saddle and did a few other things. We went directly back to the clinic.

My riding leg felt a great deal heavier than my first prosthesis—weighing a good 15 pounds, and it wasn't what you could call pretty either. But, as Fred reasoned, why should I go to the expense of having it covered with foam and cosmetically designed, when all I was going to do was use it for horseback riding. After all, one usually wears pants while riding.

Satisfied with all the adjustments, we went back to the stable on my last day in Los Angeles. Fred assisted me, with the help of the stable owner, onto the back of a big old gentle mare. Once I eased myself into the saddle, I was able to sit upright. Fred bent my knee up where it hung inches from the horse's mouth. I couldn't get the foot into the stirrup because it didn't have enough flexion.

Once I was settled on the horse's back, in a reasonably comfortable position, I kicked her into a slow walk. It had been over a year since I had been on a horse, and I had so looked forward to the occasion. But I didn't have time to enjoy the ride. I was too scared, too panicky. The sensation of sitting on the back of a tall horse without the natural balance of my real leg was a frightening feeling.

The "dummy," hanging close enough to the horse's mouth for her to bite if she wished, offered a certain amount of weight and balance, but it was still unnatural for me not to have the foot in the stirrup. I missed not being able to hug the horse with my two legs. I rode for only a few minutes and then said that I was ready to get off. Fred could sense my uneasiness and said that time and practice was all that I needed to build up my confidence. The prosthesis will work, he said. I just had to re-educate myself on how to ride a horse.

I found that I could get off the horse by myself by merely slipping my good leg out of the stirrup and bringing it over the back of the horse. I lay over the horse's back on my stomach and guided myself down, making sure that the knee was locked securely before I hit the ground on both feet. Today I am able to use my walking leg to ride a horse. But I will always require assistance to mount.

After Christianna and I came home from Hollywood, my riding leg took my first leg's original place in the corner of the room. And just like my first leg, I left it standing there, totally abandoned. Tony called a couple of days after I returned and said that he wanted to come over and see what Karg had come up with for horseback riding. When he arrived later that afternoon, he barely said hello. He brushed right past me heading for the living room, where he somehow knew he would find the leg. After inspecting it curiously he turned to me and said, "When do we go for a ride?"

"Oh, I don't know. Next week, maybe."

"Next week," Tony repeated. "What's wrong with tomorrow?"

"Tomorrow?" I yelled out a little too loudly. "Tomorrow's a bit too soon, don't you think?"

"Too soon? Too soon for what? You said you've already tried it out in Hollywood. Right?"

"Well, yes. But I only rode for a few minutes and in a small area."

"All the more reason then to try it again and not wait too long. It's just like being thrown off a horse—if you don't get right back on you never will. Besides, at our place you'll have 8000 acres to ride on."

Tony and his son Greg had been keeping my horse at their ranch for the past month and riding her daily in an effort to calm her down for me. She hadn't been ridden in over a year, so she was even more squirrely than usual. She was a barrel racing horse and her high spirit, which had always excited me and which had been necessary for competition, now needed tempering if I wished to continue riding her. Tony and Greg had somehow managed to do this.

I finally agreed to go to Tony's place the following day. It's one thing to say to yourself and everyone else that you're going to ride again, but it's another thing when it comes right down to doing it. I forced myself to put my heavy riding leg on the following morning. Walking with the new leg was much more difficult than with my other leg, because of its weight and its flexive knee action. But once I got on the horse it wouldn't make any difference.

When I arrived at the Costa ranch, I was surprised to see Missy already saddled and waiting patiently in the corral. I went into the house to the kitchen where Ann and Tony were drinking coffee. Excitedly, I began to throw questions at Tony. "How did you train Missy to stand in one place? How come she's not stomping the ground and dancing around, like she used to whenever I tied her up?"

Tony explained how he and Greg had worked with her every day trying to calm her down and how he now felt that she would be perfectly safe for me to ride. I finished my first cup of coffee and then asked for a second. Then a third. I was stalling for time.

Tony finally said, "Let's go, Lenor! Let's get your butt back in the saddle."

Up until that moment I had been so confident, so optimistic that I would ride again that I not only had myself believing it, but everyone else as well. But that afternoon as Tony was helping me get on Missy's back, I began to have second thoughts. "What if Missy falls? How will I jump off? What if the "dummy" gets hung up in the saddle and Missy panics and runs off dragging me?"

"Oh, my God, I don't think I can go through with this," I said aloud.

"Calm down, Lenor. I'm right here, and Missy is behaving perfectly."

Tony was right. Missy used to take off whenever I got

ready to mount her, sometimes even before I had my foot in the stirrup—a bad habit I had let her get into but never tried to break because I enjoyed being able to run along side of her and then leap onto her back.

Also, she should have been fidgeting because I was mounting her on the opposite side from the one she was used to. (One normally mounts a horse on the left side.) I had to get on the wrong side because I had to use the strength of my good leg to stand in the stirrup and swing into the saddle. But in order to reach up high enough, Tony had to cup his hands and place them under my good foot. With my one foot secure in his hands, I shifted my weight to the bad leg. I grabbed for the saddle horn and the back of the saddle. Tony boosted my foot up to the stirrup and quickly pushed my prosthesis over the back of the horse, then ran around to the left side and pulled it forward in a natural riding position. Once I was situated in the saddle, my original optimism slowly began to return.

The first thing Tony noticed and didn't like was the way in which my fake leg hung on the left side. He thought that maybe he could make something that would hold the leg in place, offering a little more stability, but yet wouldn't let me get caught in the saddle if I should happen to fall.

He took a crescent-shaped piece of iron, padded it with foam rubber, and then wrapped it with electrical tape. He then tied a piece of rawhide to the middle of the iron crescent and fastened the other end to the saddle tree. I could rest the thigh of my fake leg in the curve and bear down on it for balance. Yet it would allow me to fall free of the horse if I should fall. With my prosthesis established in the sling, I was able to maintain a straight sitting position in the saddle.

The corral I was riding in was too small. I asked Tony

if I could ride in the bigger corral. He was concerned at first because the other corral had a definite slope and he was afraid that I might fall forward or to the right. He agreed to let me move only after I convinced him that I was balanced sufficiently enough in the saddle to compensate for the sloping terrain.

To make up for my imbalance and to keep the saddle from shifting to the right, I had to keep throwing my body weight to the left. After about thirty minutes of practicing in the larger corral, my confidence had grown enough to announce, "I'm ready, Tony, open the gate!"

"Wait! I'll get my horse and ride out with you." On the outside chance that we would be riding together that afternoon, Tony had already saddled his horse. He opened the gate and we rode out. Another barrier had been broken.

As we rode out of the confines of the corral, I felt an exhilarating sense of freedom. It was so easy. For the first time since my amputation I was moving gracefully, effortlessly along dirt paths, over rocks, bushes, squirrel holes, going up and down ditch banks, through puddles of water—all the things that were tremendous obstacles to me when walking. It didn't matter that I had to be on the back of a four-legged beast in order to do these things. It only mattered that I was doing them and covering ground at the same time.

"I can do anything now," I thought to myself. "Run, jump, climb, cover great distances."

As we rode, neither of us felt it necessary to speak. I was alone in my thoughts yet keenly aware of the elements surrounding me. The slight breeze kissing my face, the sun burning my back, the dust, the heat. It was springtime. The rolling hills were green. Wild flowers were blooming. The sky was cloudless, blue, and bright.

As we rode silently, side by side, I could smell the

185

delicious intermingling aromas of horseflesh and leather. I could feel the quivering, powerful yet sensitive muscles of the horse beneath me, awaiting my slightest command. I slightly nudged Missy's ribs and in one explosive force she lunged into a gallop. Tony followed. As I hung on for dear life riding to the top of the hill, tears mixed with sweat and dirt came streaming down my face. When we reached the crest of the hill and brought our horses to a halt, I looked back at Tony for some sign of approval. From the moisture blinding his eyes, I could tell that he was more than satisfied.

My friends then and today wonder why I take the risks that are involved in riding a horse—why it is so important to me. Aside from just plain enjoying horseback riding, it gives me a chance to be physically involved in a sport. I can't play tennis, baseball, volleyball, or other sports that I used to enjoy; but I can ride a horse. I don't have to feel sorry for myself whenever my husband sets up a tennis match with some of our friends. I just go for a horseback ride.

Before Christianna was born, I used to ride alone on the ranch, sometimes packing a picnic in my saddle bags and riding out to where Joseph was working. I used to daydream about one day having children and teaching them how to ride a horse and how they would join me on picnics and long rides out to meet their father in the fields. When Christianna was born I was impatient for her to reach an age when she could learn how to ride. After her second birthday, we got her a pony for Christmas and I taught her to ride. We rode together. My dream had partially come true.

After my surgery, I felt that Daniella had been cheated. How could I teach her to ride a horse now that she was finally old enough? However, after that glorious afternoon riding up at the Costa's ranch, I was able to fulfill my dreams of having both children ride with me.

Joseph isn't much for pleasure riding, but he likes working cattle, roping, and rodeo competition. Whenever he's doing one of these things, I tag along on my horse. It affords me an opportunity to be with him and participate.

I know that it is extremely dangerous for an amputee to ride a horse. I won't try to diminish that fact. But a few things I've learned I think lessen that danger. I do not strap myself to the saddle, or strap a foot in the stirrup. I try constantly to balance myself, compensating with my body for whatever is missing. And I ride only a well-trained, calm horse.

There are risks involved even when extensive precautions are taken. But for me, the reward of being physically active in a sport far outweighs the risks. Today, I'm able to participate in many other sports besides horseback riding.

Bicycling—on a three wheeler—with a small motor attached to the front wheel, that takes me up to twenty miles per hour. All I have to do is pump for a while with my right foot, until I get it going fast enough to engage the starting mechanism of the engine.

Water skiing. The first time I got up on one water ski I surprised everyone, including myself. I had never skied on one ski before, even when I had two legs. I began on a six-foot O'Brien ski, which is shaped almost like a banana and has a slalom fin. On the second try I got up. As I skied for three miles over the glass smooth San Joaquin Delta waterways, my friends cheering me on, I shouted, "Thank you. Thank you, dear God for another miracle. I can't believe this is happening to me—I'm actually skiing!"

In the winter, in the seat of a snowmobile, I can be out in the snow feeling the cold, experiencing the blinding rays that bounce off the snow and feeling the icy snow burning my face as I reach speeds of up to fifty miles per hour. Balance is vitally important in the guiding of a snowmobile. Whenever I'm confronted with a steep cliff and it is necessary to make a sharp left turn, I have to throw my body forcibly from my right side to the left in order to negotiate the turn. But I manage it, even with one of my daughters riding behind me.

That first year when I was trying to adjust to living a normal life, I found myself trying to adjust to a new career as well. One morning a local radio announcer asked me to appear on his talk show and discuss "Coping." I agreed and was subsequently hired to voice some commercials. Within a short time I was recording a five-minute weekly show on fashion. By summer my five-minute show had turned into a thirty-minute talk show on which I inter- viewed local personalities. By fall I was interviewing better-known celebrities.

After about six months with the station I was forced to give up my column and fashion shows because of the heavy broadcasting schedule. I was delighted with my new role of interviewer through which I could enter different persons' lives each week, and be stimulated by their diverse and often fascinating careers.

I often thought how lucky I was to have had experience that suited me for this. It would have been impossible if my previous talents had been of a more physical nature. What if I had been a ballet dancer, or a physical education teacher? The loss of my leg would have prevented me from ever returning to my career. Radio not only offered me exciting work, but it was also physically possible for me to assume this career. Another blessing.

Moments

Trying to fill the space
That emptiness takes
Trying to find the place
That hopelessness makes.

That first year I was able to accomplish all the things I had set out to do. I proved to everyone including myself that I could still do almost everything that I used to do. But it was too much.

My family did not expect me to be "wonder woman," nor did my friends; but I expected it of myself. My greatest fear, after I lost my leg, was that someone might say, "Oh, remember all the things Lenor used to do? What a pity she can no longer take care of herself or her family. I feel so sorry for her kids and her husband. Don't you?"

I was determined to hear praise from others, instead of seeing pity on their faces. In a year's time I was able to hear, "How can Lenor do everything she does? Why she actually does more than I do, and I have two legs!"

That's what I wanted and needed to hear. It boosted my ego and afforded me the confidence required for me to carry on my life normally. However, by the end of that year I was ready for a physical breakdown. I was worn out. I realized that if I wanted to continue doing the things that really mattered to me, I would have to rearrange my priorities. I would have to do only the important things; not do anything and everything just to impress others.

If I wanted to go dancing with my husband on a Saturday night, I would relax that day and not sap my energy with grocery shopping or general house cleaning. I learned to shop the day before and maybe clean the house the day after so that I could be rested for the dance. If I want to do some baking, I do it in the morning because I'm rested. While I'm at the kitchen sink standing and waiting for the cookies to bake, I organize dinner. I clean the upstairs rooms of the house just after I've finished with my morning bath and dressing. Then, I'm prepared to go downstairs for the rest of the day.

Probably the most important decision I had to make was whether or not to go ahead with a sterilization procedure. I hadn't agreed to the minor surgery because I still harbored the notion of another pregnancy. I relented only after I realized that it was much more important that I be a healthy wife and mother for my present family. If I became pregnant I would have to spend months bedridden, and even at that, Dr. Glover said that he would not guarantee my life or the baby's life. So I dismissed the futile notion and went ahead with the tubal ligation.

It's difficult, yes, to do everything that I used to do. I cannot deny that fact. I never take a step that is not painful, or not a well-calculated move. Whenever I want to go to the kitchen or upstairs I must plan how many steps it will take and if it would be easier to go first to the kitchen, then go upstairs, or vice versa. I sometimes wonder why I don't become depressed, knowing that I will always have to plan each step I take, knowing that it will always be difficult for me just to walk.

I think the only reason I don't let it get me down is because I don't dwell on it. Rose Kennedy, when once asked how she could accept all the tragedies that had occurred in her life, explained, "Self-pity takes so much time, and really I don't have the time." Like Mrs. Kennedy, I don't have the time either.

Friends, suspicious of my sunny disposition, sometimes will seriously probe, "There must be days, Lenor, when you are really down—really depressed." To my friends I confide that there are moments of depression in my life—but not days, not hours, and not minutes—only moments.

Moments, when I pass a shop window and see a reflection of a woman walking with an obvious limp. Why is she limping, I ask myself, and why must she use a cane when she appears no older than me?

Moments, when at night, after I've taken off my prosthesis and happen to pass by a mirror and see a figure on crutches. It's very difficult for me to identify with the reflection. After all, I have never once in my life had to use crutches.

Moments, when at night I hear one of my daughters cry out. Instinctively, I jump up and start to run to her. Just before I take that fatal step I realize that I can't run to my daughter—no matter how much she might need me.

Moments, when I am in bed and my head turns to the side of the dresser, where two crutches lean, waiting. At first, in my drowsiness, I think that I must have hurt my foot in an accident, perhaps while dancing. "Oh yes, I was out dancing the other night and someone got a little boisterous and accidentally kicked me"; and then it all comes back.

Moments, when one of my girlfriends brings out a shining new pair of high-heeled shoes with the extra thin heel and the ribbon thin straps;

Moments, when a girlfriend models for my approval one of her slinky new dresses, saying she wouldn't dream of wearing a slip underneath for fear of a seam line showing through;

Moments, when I yearn to run in my husband's fields, on the beach, or in the back yard with my children;

Moments, when my mother looks at me with an expression of bewilderment that says, "Why did it have to happen to my little girl?"

Moments, when I have an overwhelming desire to walk gracefully, effortlessly, and with just a wee shake of my fanny;

Moments, when I'm without my prosthesis and something I need is just a few steps away;

Moments, when I'm sitting and waiting for a friend

in a hotel lobby and I catch an attractive man staring at me. My friend arrives. I must get up and walk;

Moments, when I dream that I have two legs, and then I wake up.

The moments when I experience the deepest depression are the moments when my husband and I get into some little argument, and he leaves the house before we have had a chance to resolve our differences. I can't run after him to catch him to explain my side of the argument— I'm left alone.

Self-pity engulfs me. It's during these moments that my condition suddenly comes tumbling down on me, rocking me, shaking me, and finally leaves me wailing.

A foreign cry escapes from somewhere deep within. It's ghostly, eerie, it's as if it's coming from someone else. The wailing leaves me frightened because of its screeching high pitch, its strangeness, its intensity. Ancient Greek women wailed when mourning a death. I wonder if those moments when I'm wailing are moments that my subconscious is mourning the death of my leg.

As the months pass and my accomplishments multiply, I think often about my *promessa* and wonder if I can ever do enough to fulfill it. And then I notice that over the past 5 years, opportunities to do so have presented themselves almost from the beginning, even though I may not have recognized them at the time.

It was during that month of waiting to go shopping for a leg that local churches began asking me to give my testimony at their Sunday services. I really didn't know what giving one's testimony actually meant.

"Just speak about your circumstances," Reverend Stan Davis explained to me. "And tell how your faith gave you strength to see you through."

Deep down somewhere in the inner recesses of my

heart I didn't want to speak or give my testimony about what happened to me. It meant reliving the grief of the past two months. I didn't want to subject myself to the possibility of emotionally breaking down in front of a whole congregation as I told my story. I asked myself, "If I can't even reread the letters I received in the hospital, then how will I be able to expound on my circumstances, and how will it benefit these people? For what reason should I stand on one leg in front of a church full of people and relate my story? For what purpose?"

I accepted Reverend Davis' proposal only after I remembered my *promessa*. Perhaps God wanted me to speak out on how I was able to adjust to my circumstances through my faith in Him and to offer hope and inspiration to others. I had to go. I couldn't take the chance that God, in anger, might back out of our bargain.

As I stood at the pulpit, supported only by the strength of my one remaining leg and God's will, I spoke on how I was able to survive physically and emotionally, through God, the most terrifying experience of my life. The words came easily—unrestrained. I explained how, through prayer, I was better able to cope with my phantom pain; how I was able to get off drugs "cold turkey"; and how I was better able to adjust to my fate.

After the services, a lady came up to me and told me that she was undergoing treatments for cancer. After seeing and listening to me that morning, she said, she felt renewed hope for her own recovery. I had inspired her to fight her disease, instead of giving in to it. She said that if I could continue on with my life, courageously, on one leg, then she too could continue on with her life and accept the rigors of cancer therapy and, hopefully, win her battle against the disease as well.

This was an entirely new and awesome position—to be thought of as brave, courageous, inspirational. I had never in my life enjoyed such high regard. I realized that in some small way I had touched many people with my short talk. I decided I would speak to groups again whenever I could.

Through friends and neighbors, I have also met and talked to many people who had recently lost a limb. One girl had lost her leg in an accident when she was helping her boyfriend change a tire. Her boyfriend had left her soon afterward, and she was sinking deeper and deeper into depression. At first, she was withdrawn, but after a while she opened up to me and started talking about her accident, her boyfriend, and her missing leg. I could feel her relief at having someone who could identify with her, someone who could understand her loss. There is nothing in this world more consoling than talking with another person who has survived a similar catastrophe.

A friend who is a lawyer asked me to visit one of her clients—a young prostitute who had lost her leg because of a shotgun wound. She was also a heroin addict. Terry related to me at once when I told her of my drug addiction and how I was able to beat it. I told her that if she ever expected to walk again, she needed all of her faculties. She could not afford to be on something that would impair her vision, her coordination, her balance, her will. Two months after her surgery, I saw Terry again. She was still on crutches waiting to be fitted for a prosthesis. She told me that she had kicked her drug habit, and from her healthy appearance I believed her.

I also met a woman who had a malignant tumor high on her thigh and was faced with the most difficult choice of her life: an operation on the tumor, which would involve severing the major nerves to the leg, massive x-ray treatments and a high risk of the cancer spreading; or a hemipelvectomy, with a 90 percent chance of cure. I refrained from making any recommendation—the decision had to be hers. Betty had opted for the operation, but after seeing me and witnessing all the things that I could do, she decided to let them amputate.

"I don't want to dance, ride horses, ride bicycles, or model," she said to me. "I just want to walk." When she told her doctors about me, they exclaimed, "Impossible! Hemipelvectomies do not walk, much less ride horses."

Today Betty is reasonably sure that she's cured of cancer, and she walks.

Perhaps it is in these ways that I am working on my *promessa* and making my achievements benefit other lives besides my own.

I returned to Mayo Clinic in June, 1978, to receive a check-up and to meet with Dr. Lowery and check the medical information in this book.

After a beautiful flight over the Rocky Mountains we arrived in Denver where we would catch a connecting flight. Everything went wrong. The electric cart passed me up in favor of a group of elderly and disabled because I didn't appear to be handicapped severely enough. I had to walk a mile to the departure gate, and the delay resulted in our losing our places on the plane. Storms forced the next plane we took to land in Minneapolis, and we had to rent a car and drive to Rochester. I had only a couple of hours to sleep before my first appointment at Mayo. I had so wanted to look and feel my best for this return visit.

Rochester looked like a different city to me. It was summertime and everything was emerald green. The huge old trees that line the streets were full of foliage. Flowers bloomed everywhere.

The first morning back in Rochester, Evie picked me up and took me to the clinic, where I was scheduled for tests before meeting with Dr. Lowery. As I stood before the massive doors that lead into the Mayo Clinic, I hesitated before going in, wondering how I would react once I reentered its vast domain.

I took a long deep breath and stepped in. The emotional impact of actually walking into the clinic on my own two feet, after the horrendous experience of being wheeled out four years before, will probably remain with me forever.

When I had completed the necessary tests, Evie suggested that we go over to the hotel for breakfast. We went through the underground passageways that connected the clinic with the hotel. As we walked through the maze of tunnels, I asked Evie if she was sure that these were the same ones we had gone through five years ago. She said they were.

"But how could they be?" I thought to myself. "Those tunnels were dark and foreboding. These are bright and cheerful. The walls are gleaming with colorful ceramic tiles and look at all these helpful signs to guide and direct." After we had gone through the underground tunnels and entered the hotel I commented to Evie on what an elegant, charming hotel it was, with its glossy hardwood floors and beautiful wood paneling. Evie politely reminded me that this was the same hotel that Joseph and I had moved out of because I had thought it drab and depressing.

At one o'clock I was to meet with Dr. Lowery. I carefully selected my prettiest pantsuit. I was anxious to please him, first, with how I looked and, second, with how I could walk. The last time he had seen me I was swollen and bandaged, and the only way I could get around was either on crutches or in a wheelchair.

The nurse led me to a little cubicle that was identical to the one I had waited in before. The view from the window, however, was different, and so was the waiting.

I was unaccountably nervous. Dr. Lowery and another young doctor briskly entered the room. I wanted to jump up and throw my arms around this man who had saved my life. But Dr. Lowery greeted me with only a cursory nod and a tight smile. I sat tensely in my seat.

My tests were absolutely clear, he reported. I was, in his opinion, cured of cancer the day he operated. Before I'd had a chance to savor that glorious information, Dr. Lowery abruptly changed the subject and asked me about my book. He said that he had already read the first two chapters. He was disturbed by my negative remarks about Mayo, Rochester, the subway system, the prestigious Kahler Hotel, and asked, "Where's this deserted dairy, that looms dark and empty in the distance outside St. Marys Hospital anyway? That's a monastery."

I was momentarily speechless. A monastery! I remembered the grim, dark shapes of the buildings and all the feelings I had had while lying in that hospital room began to come back. I realized that I had seen everything through eyes of fear, and that what I had seen in the short time since my arrival this morning showed how my vision had been transformed. *I* had been transformed. Couldn't Dr. Lowery see that, looking at me sitting in front of him, well dressed and walking on my own?

As I tried to make him understand my mental attitude four years earlier, I could feel myself slowly, irreversibly losing control. Tears began to trickle down my face. Dr. Lowery and the other doctor gazed at me stonily. I tried to compose myself, but as I continued explaining, tears were no longer trickling down my face—they were pouring.

Dr. Lowery and the other doctor both clumsily offered me their handkerchiefs. Dr. Lowery, now visibly upset, asked if he had said or done something wrong, and if so, he was very sorry. I looked at him. He really did not seem to know what I was feeling.

"No, no, Dr. Lowery," I assured him. "I'm just exhausted from the trip."

I then proceeded to tell him about our frustrating delays en route. When I had finished, Dr. Lowery, infuriated that one of his patients was ignored, seized the telephone, called up an executive of the airlines, and berated him for several minutes. After this emotional venting, Dr. Lowery relaxed and we were able to re-establish our old rapport.

I walked around for him. Both doctors were amazed by my mobility, by my ability to walk in a nearly normal manner, and by the design of my prosthesis. After I went through my routine—sitting, bending, dancing—Dr. Lowery asked if I would come back again the next day to visit the rehabilitation center and meet with some of the doctors, physical therapists, prosthetists, and patients. He mentioned that the letters I had periodically sent him describing my progress had been very impressive to the operating crews.

"As you can imagine," he said, "they see the patient in the operating room, but they very rarely see them after surgery."

He felt that my appearance at the rehabilitation center "would serve a good purpose." I agreed to return.

I took the elevator down to the first floor with the biggest, silliest grin on my face. I greeted everyone, smiled at everyone. "Have a good day. Have a nice day," I said. I found myself accidentally bumping into visitors and patients; some of the latter in wheelchairs, some with sores on their bodies, some with hair missing, some arthritics laboriously trying to walk, and some on gurneys.

"Oops, excuse me. Oh, excuse me. I'm sorry. Have a nice day." I was giggling, I was laughing, I was crying.

As I walked toward the enticing glass doors, with my clean bill of health tucked under my arm, I could see the little park across the street that innocently covered the vast subterranean radiation center. When I swung the doors open, momentarily blinded by the brilliant sunshine, I could contain my exuberance no longer—in spite of what I had just left behind, in spite of what was under the green grass across the way, in spite of the fact that I had to return the next day (it just might be one more way of fulfilling my *promessa*). Unabashedly, I looked up to the sky and thanked God for my reprieve—for each and every moment.